Sh

Leadership
FOR

DUMMIES®

PORTABLE EDITION

Leadership
FOR
DUMMIES®
PORTABLE EDITION

by Dr John Marrin

A John Wiley and Sons, Ltd, Publication

Leadership For Dummies,® Portable Edition

Published by
John Wiley & Sons, Ltd
The Atrium
Southern Gate
Chichester
West Sussex
PO19 8SQ
England

Email (for orders and customer service enquires): cs-books@wiley.co.uk

Visit our Home Page on www.wileyeurope.com

Copyright © 2011 John Wiley & Sons, Ltd, Chichester, West Sussex, England

Published by John Wiley & Sons, Ltd, Chichester, West Sussex

Wiley also publishes its books in a variety of electronic formats. Some content that appears in print may not be available in electronic books.

British Library Cataloguing in Publication Data: A catalogue record for this book is available from the British Library.

ISBN: 978-1-119-97445-1 (paperback), 978-1-119-97499-4 (ebook), 978-1-119-97500-7 (ebook), 978-1-119-97501-4 (ebook)

Printed and bound in Great Britain by CPI Antony Rowe, Chippenham, Wiltshire

10 9 8 7 6 5 4 3 2 1

WILEY

About the Author

Dr John Marrin is an expert on how leaders of organisations totally engage their directors, managers and employees to enhance their commitment and achieve higher levels of individual, team and business performance. He is a leadership coach and organisation development specialist to a wide range of clients including large multinationals, privately owned businesses and public sector organisations. While working primarily with organisations throughout the United Kingdom, John is also experienced in supporting clients in Europe and South America.

John is intensely enthusiastic about engaging people to work better together through enhancing mutual understanding and establishing shared commitment and accountability for achieving success: he redefined the meaning and practice of engaging through his DPhil. John is a Chartered Fellow of the Chartered Institute of Personnel and Development, and holds a Master of Arts in Management Learning from Lancaster University.

John is founder of Marwel & Co. which specialises in leadership development and employee engagement. To find out more about the services of Marwel & Co., visit his website: www.marwel-co.com. John's email address is jmarrin@marwel-co.com.

Dedication

I dedicate this book to my wife Linda, and my sons, Paul and David, who have given me the inspiration, encouragement and support to clarify and fulfil my vocation.

Author's Acknowledgements

My special thanks go to my wife and sons for putting up with seeing much less of me during the process of writing this book, and to my wider family and friends for their tolerance. You have all been much neglected, but not forgotten, for many months. I also want to acknowledge my parents, John and Vera, for encouraging me and instilling values that I continue to cherish.

Thanks to the team at Wiley, especially David Palmer for inviting me to write this book, to Rachael Chilvers for guiding and supporting me throughout the process, and to Andy Finch for helping me to clarify my thinking.

I thank my clients and colleagues for the opportunities to work and learn with you, and for the experiences that have eventually been distilled into the contents of this book.

Publisher's Acknowledgements

We're proud of this book; please send us your comments through our Dummies online registration form located at www.dummies.com/register/.

Some of the people who helped bring this book to market include the following:

Acquisitions, Editorial and Media Development

Project Editor: Rachael Chilvers

Development Editor: Andy Finch

Commissioning Editor: David Palmer

Technical Editor: Richard Pettinger, Business Management lecturer, UCL

Proofreader: Kim Vernon

Assistant Editor: Ben Kemble

Production Manager: Daniel Mersey

Cover Photo: © Steve Hamblin / Alamy

Cartoons: Ed McLachlan

Composition Services

Project Coordinator: Kristie Rees

Layout and Graphics: Christin Swinford

Proofreader: Rebecca Denoncour

Indexer: Potomac Indexing, LLC

Contents at a Glance

Table of Contents

Chapter 5: Employing the Power of Engaging Leadership 85

Chapter 6: Becoming an Engaging Leader 101

Introduction

• •

*L*eadership is something that you recognise when you see it and notice when you don't see it, and yet most people find it hard to articulate what leadership really *is*. I've written this book because I want to remove the mystique of leadership and enable you to ground leadership in your everyday work practice.

Every chapter in this book is designed to help you to understand different aspects of leadership and how to lead in different contexts and situations. The information you find within the covers of this book is grounded in the real world. This information is primarily distilled from my working with thousands of leaders in many different types of organisations, including owner-managed and public limited companies, public sector organisations and charities. I coached and mentored leaders, built high-performing work teams, worked through difficult leadership dilemmas and facilitated senior management teams to transform their organisations.

About This Book

Reading this book enables you to discover how to work on becoming the great leader you aspire to be (who aspires to be an average leader?). If you're new to the world of leadership, you can find all you need to succeed in your new position. If you're an experienced leader, I challenge you to turn the kaleidoscope, and look at your leadership philosophy and practice from a new perspective to identify what's working for you – and the people you lead – and what's not.

You can make the fastest progress in enhancing your leadership skills by putting what you learn into practice, and then reflecting on and learning more from your experiences.

Leadership in a work setting is all about engaging people and gaining their commitment to making a highly valued contribution to improving the performance and success of their organisation, and enable them to gain a real sense of fulfilment through doing so. Among the topics covered in this book are:

- ✓ How leading and managing people are different.
- ✓ How to gain the commitment of people who work for and with you.
- ✓ Why you have to start with leading yourself.
- ✓ How to succeed in leading people through change.
- ✓ How to increase your influence in your organisation.
- ✓ How to challenge people whose behaviour or performance doesn't meet your standards.
- ✓ How to lead your team.
- ✓ How to build a great senior leadership team.

I do my best to explain these things, and much more, clearly and concisely. Now that you have an insight into the content of this book, I hope you're raring to go!

Conventions Used in This Book

To help you navigate through this book, I've set up a few conventions:

- ✓ *Italic* is used for emphasis and to highlight new words or terms that I define.
- ✓ **Boldfaced** text is used to highlight important text in lists.
- ✓ `Monofont` is used for web and email addresses.

Also, I use the term *organisation* quite loosely. I define an *organisation* as a group of people who have formally come together to achieve objectives. Many different types of organisations exist, including small owner-managed businesses, global public limited companies, charities, public sector organisations and so on. I use the term *organisation* (or sometimes *company*) to refer to the business, charity or whatever that you work for.

What You're Not to Read

I've written this book so that you can easily access and understand what you want to find out about leadership in a work context. I've made it easy for you to identify material that you don't absolutely have to read. This information is interesting stuff, and you can benefit from it, but it isn't essential for you to know:

- ✔ **Text in sidebars:** The sidebars are shaded boxes that share interesting stories about real life examples to illustrate points made elsewhere in the text, but you can skip them if you wish.

- ✔ **The stuff on the copyright page:** You'll find nothing here of value unless you're looking for legal notices and reprint information! If you are, then this is the place to look.

Foolish Assumptions

I wrote this book assuming some things about you:

- ✔ You're enthusiastic about developing your leadership ability.

- ✔ You want to improve your own and others' performance.

- ✔ You've some experience of leadership through coming into contact with good or bad leaders, or through the position you currently hold in your organisation or positions you've held in the past.

- ✔ You want to know what works. While you want to understand key concepts about leadership, you're more interested in a pragmatic and practical approach to becoming the leader you aspire to be.

- ✔ You like discovering *why* as well as *what*. That is, you want to know *why* people typically do what they do at work rather than just knowing *what* they do.

- ✔ You want to make a positive difference and contribution to the organisation you work for and the people you work with.

How This Book Is Organised

I've organised this book into five parts to make the material easier to understand and access by keeping related material together. Each part is broken down into chapters, and the table of contents gives you details on each chapter.

Part 1: Introducing Leadership and Leading Yourself

In this part, you find the key differences between leading and managing people and start to identify your own leadership strengths and development needs. I introduce you to the notion of being an authentic leader, and explain why working on leading yourself is critical to becoming the leader you aspire to be. You discover how to learn more about leadership from reflecting on your experiences. You find out how to identify the values that are really important to you and how these may impact on how you lead people.

Part II: Leading Others

To be a successful leader, others have to choose to follow you. I explain how you can really engage people so that they give you their commitment: they put all the effort, knowledge, expertise, and skills they have into doing a great job rather than just being compliant. You find out about leadership styles and how to choose the most appropriate style for different situations. I emphasise why you have to consciously set the standards that you expect people to work to, and you discover how to effectively challenge people who don't meet your standards.

Part III: Leading People Through Change

In this part, I introduce you to approaches to implementing change in teams and organisations that enable people to embrace change. You also find techniques for embedding new ways of working, and how to prevent people from slipping back into old habits.

Part IV: Leading Teams

This part is where you find out about leading teams, and the challenges that you may experience. You discover the characteristics that separate great teams from good ones, and how you can build a high-performing team. I provide tips on how to create a senior leadership team that's a great role model for everyone in the organisation.

Part V: The Part of Tens

When you're looking for a quick reminder of good leadership practice or a bit of inspiration, you can find it here. This part directs you to ten tips on taking the lead and leading people.

Icons Used in This Book

The icons in this book point out particular kinds of information that you may find useful. Here's an explanation of what each icon stands for:

Take particular notice of the text next to this icon because it provides advice on how to become an exceptional leader.

This icon is a friendly reminder of important points to take note of.

This icon highlights practical advice that you can use to lead people in a wide range of work situations.

This icon highlights real-life stories about leadership that I hope you find inspiring or useful.

Discover exercises to help you to explore leadership next to this icon.

Watch out! If you don't heed the advice next to this icon, you may end up facing a worse situation.

Where to Go from Here

You don't have to read this book from cover to cover as you can get most benefit from it by going though it in the order and at a pace that's right for you. I organise the contents of this book to enable *you* to take the lead. You can take a structured, sequential approach or read the chapters in any order; immediately diving into a section to find out what you need to know to deal with a situation or problem you're experiencing.

Use the table of contents to see what you're attracted to first. For example, if you want to know the main differences between leading and managing, go to Chapter 1. Or if you'd like to hone your skills in encouraging people to work to your standards turn to Chapter 8.

Regardless of how you work your way through *Leadership For Dummies*, I'm sure that you'll become the great leader you aspire to be. I'm enthusiastic about helping people to become great leaders so if you've any specific questions or comments, please feel free to visit my website at www.marwel-co.com.

Here's to your ongoing success!

Part I

Introducing Leadership and Leading Yourself

'So you think you were born to be a leader, Mauleverer?'

In this part . . .

The chapters in this part help you to acquire an understanding of the key differences between leading and managing people, and lay the foundations for you becoming the great leader you aspire to be. You start to work on developing your leadership ability by initially focusing on leading yourself, and you find techniques on how to learn more about leadership from your experiences. You spend time on clarifying the values that are most important to you and how these guide your behaviour in leading people.

Chapter 1

Leadership and Management: Two Sides of the Same Coin

. . . .

In This Chapter

▶ Making sense of your experiences of being led and managed

▶ Getting to grips with changing leadership and management roles

▶ Appreciating the key differences between leading and managing

▶ Earning the right to lead

. . . .

*L*eadership is common sense; but unfortunately not always common practice. With the right information gleaned from my experience of working closely with thousands of managers, and some practice and thought on your part, leading can become as natural as riding a bike (even if you do experience a few wobbles along the way)!

If you couple your common sense to this book's numerous tips, prompts, guidelines, memory joggers and even (dare I say it) pearls of wisdom, you can become the great leader you aspire to be. You can literally get your ducks in a row – just like on the front cover – reflected by your staff wanting to follow you without you having to look behind to check whether they're still there. Carry out the exercises and implement the advice throughout the book, and you can turn effective leadership into your personal common practice. You start by looking into the practices of leadership and management.

Some people strongly argue that 'leadership' and 'management' are different practices, whereas others see them as simply different aspects of the same thing. Although many boffins may think otherwise, this question is far too important to leave to academics – after all, leadership and management are part of everyday life!

So, what do you think? Don't worry if you're unsure about how to answer this question at the moment, after reading the guidance and information I provide in this chapter, your answer will be as clear as the nose on your face. For now, however, take the hint from the chapter title: I see leadership and management as two complementary aspects of the same overall discipline.

In this chapter, I help you sort through the maze of your personal experiences of being led and managed, so that you can distil your thinking and decide on how you view leadership and management. You get to compare your significant experiences with the information I provide and by doing so clarify what leadership and management involves, what you expect of leaders – yourself and those leading you – and the key differences between the two practices.

In addition, you can use the outcomes from the exercises in this chapter to develop your leadership ability when working on leading yourself in Chapters 2 and 3.

Considering Your Experiences of Leadership and Management

Ever since you were a baby you've been experiencing leadership and management, although you weren't conscious of doing so then! As a small child, no doubt you started to notice aspects of leadership and management as regards how you were brought up – and you won't have enjoyed all of those experiences because, for example, you didn't always get what you wanted. These early insights are significant in developing your personal idea of leaders and managers.

Your parents or guardians were leading and managing you through your childhood and adolescence, and even into your adult life if they're anything like my mother! (She told me, virtually every time we met, that I was working too hard and advised me to slow down.) For example, by instilling certain values in you and getting you to school on time, your parents were leading and managing you.

Working through your own experiences

In this section and the next one I help you to think about your own experiences of being led and managed, so that you clarify your expectations and are able to utilise the insights you gain in working more effectively with your own leaders and the people you lead. In particular, you:

- ✔ Discover how much of an effect your experiences of leaders and managers have shaped your current thoughts about how you prefer to lead and manage people.

- ✔ Find out that you can have a significant impact on how people who work for and with you think, feel and act.

- ✔ Clarify your expectations of leaders and managers by completing a few exercises. You can use the outcomes of these exercises to think more about your strengths and development needs in leading and managing people.

Although I start this chapter by revealing that you've been experiencing leadership and management since you were a baby, I don't ask you to dredge your memories of childhood when working through your experiences. Instead, I want you to reflect on experiences that were significant to you during your formative years and adult life. Clarifying your own current thinking on leadership and management before you explore my description of what leaders and managers are expected to do is important for the following reasons:

- ✔ Building on your existing knowledge and approach helps you to understand and practise leading and managing people.

- ✔ Comparing and contrasting your views with my description of what leaders and managers are expected to do enables you to consider the implications of any similarities and differences.

- ✔ Working through your own experiences enables you to better understand leadership and management as you make sense of your personal experiences.

I suggest that you start to clarify your thinking on leadership and management by identifying any principles or values acquired during your formative years as regards how you were expected to treat people, and then describe how this experience shaped the way you treat people. The following exercise show you how.

1. **Complete Table 1-1 so that you have the information handy for future reference.**

2. **Write each 'principle' or 'value' in the first column.** It can be a phrase or saying that you recall hearing your parent or guardian say many times.

3. **Note in the second column what this item meant to you.**

4. **Write a few words to capture how each principle or value shaped how you treat people or expect to be treated by others.** I give one example to help you get started.

Table 1-1 Principles or Values Acquired through Formative Years Shape how You Treat People

Principle or Value	What This Means to You	How This Meaning Shaped How You Treat, and Expect to be Treated by, Others
Look after others and they'll look after you.	Treat people how you like to be treated.	I always strive to treat people with respect.

Your approach to working with people is likely to be significantly influenced by the content of the third column. These notes describe you and how you prefer to work with people: they're part of your 'DNA' regarding your thinking and approach to working with people. Of course, the people you work with have similar or different DNAs based on principles and values they acquire in their formative years and how they interpret them, and these similarities or differences have a big effect on how well you work together.

Just as you can improve by taking the best from the best bosses you've worked for, you also discover how you *don't* want to lead and manage from observing and working with bad bosses.

Now build on these lessons from your formative years and explore your experiences of being managed by great and bad bosses.

1. **Complete Table 1-2 so that you have the information handy for future reference.**

2. **Note the approach or behaviour you admired in the best bosses you've worked for and with in the first column.** Describe the impact or effect their approach or behaviour had on you and how you performed your job in the second column.

3. **Repeat step 2 for your experiences of working for or with bad bosses.** Note the approach or behaviour you didn't admire in the third column and its impact on you in the fourth.

Table 1-2   Summary of Good and Bad Practices I've Noticed in Great and Poor Bosses

Approach or Behaviour of Great Bosses	*Impact or Effect on How I Performed my Job*	*Approach or Behaviour of Poor Bosses*	*Impact or Effect on How I Performed my Job*
Hannah enthused about the importance of achieving our team's objectives.	I became more committed to achieving my objectives.	James didn't recognise how hard I was working.	I started to question myself about whether working all the extra hours I was doing was worthwhile.

Listing your expectations of leaders and managers

Your current understanding and approach to leading and managing people is an amalgam of who you are and the lessons you learn through your own practice as a leader and manager, and how you interpreted your experiences of other leaders and managers. You continue to develop your own approach to leading and managing people throughout your working life.

I encourage you to take the next steps on your journey by further clarifying your understanding of leadership and management by listing your expectations of leaders and managers.

1. **Go through the notes you made in column 3 in Table 1-1 and column 1 in Table 1-2.** Decide whether each point describes what you expect of a leader or manager, or both.

2. **Go through the notes you made about the approach or behaviour of poor bosses in column 3 of Table 1-2, and note the opposite of each approach or behaviour.** Decide whether each point describes what you expect of a leader or manager, or whether you think a point is relevant to leaders and managers, in which case note 'both'.

3. **Complete Table 1-3 by transferring the relevant points from steps 1 and 2 into the relevant column.** Translate each point into an action that describes what you expect a leader or manager, or both, to do.

4. **Add to your lists by noting any further expectations you have of a leader and a manager, assuming that you're working for one.**

Table 1-3 My Expectations of Leaders and Managers

I Expect Leaders to	I Expect Both Leaders and Managers to	I Expect Managers to

In the preceding exercises, you're practising the important and often underused skill of *reflecting*, in order to make sense of your experiences. (Chapter 2 has loads more details about this skill and how to enhance your ability to learn more and quicker through reflection.) Seize the opportunity now to assess how good a leader and manager you are against your current expectations by reflecting on whether you do what you expect leaders and managers to do, and whether you do it well.

My leadership strengths are:

My leadership development needs are:

My management strengths are:

My management development needs are:

If necessary, make additions to this summary after reading the next section 'Pinpointing the Differences between Leading and Managing'.

Use the Leadership Learning Plans in Chapter 2 to plan how you're going to work on your leadership and management development needs.

Pinpointing the Differences between Leading and Managing

I've led hundreds of leadership workshops and explored the differences between leading and managing with thousands of practising managers. In this section, I help you discover the key differences between leading and managing based on my experiences of coaching and working with leaders (see Figure 1-1). Numerous activities are associated with leading and managing, but I restrict my descriptions to the items that I consider to be most important.

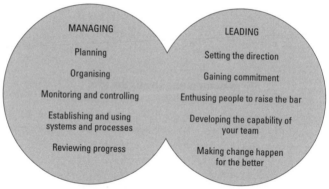

Figure 1-1: The key differences between leading and managing.

Describing the key differences

In this section, I describe some crucial differences between the activities and associated skills of leading and managing. I list the activities to reflect the general rather than absolute order in which to do them, especially for managing.

Leading involves:

✔ **Setting the direction.** Clarify the purpose of your team and how it adds value to your organisation by answering questions such as:

- Why does this team exist?

- What objectives are we expected to achieve?

- How can we achieve these objectives?

Answering these questions enables you to clarify and set the objectives that have to be achieved for your team to be successful and the main actions to take to achieve the objectives. In practice, many leaders involve members of their team in completing this analysis to enable them to:

- Create a shared sense of purpose and meaning to doing their work

- Develop a shared responsibility for the team's success

- Appreciate the team's and each individual's priorities

✔ **Gaining commitment to action.** Members of your team can deliver quite good levels of performance by complying with what you expect of them, but if you really want people to give their best you have to gain their commitment. The difference between people being committed and compliant is ownership: they take ownership for doing the task to the best of their ability rather than just doing it because you want them to. Engage individuals and the whole team through meaningful conversations about the importance of their work and gain their commitment to achieve objectives and deliver results.

✔ **Being enthusiastic about 'raising the bar'.** Enthuse about the standards of performance and behaviour you expect from your team. Question and challenge current ways of working and encourage innovation. In my experience, many teams think that they're already performing well and that they can't significantly improve their performance: they can't raise the bar!

Having a clear picture or vision about the future, including how you see the team functioning, and sharing it enthusiastically encourages members of your team to strive to improve the team's performance. Set high standards by acting with integrity and modelling the behaviours you expect from others.

✔ **Developing the capability of your team.** Act as a coach by encouraging people to be and give their best, and provide them with continual feedback. Hold individuals accountable: recognise and praise good practice, and promptly confront unacceptable performance and behaviour. Agree improvements and the support to be provided, and how to measure progress. Focus the whole team on finding better ways of working together to achieve higher levels of performance.

✔ **Making change happen for the better.** Become an active agent, rather than a victim, of change. Leading people involves having a positive impact on how they think, feel and act: and I mean people within your team and people outside of your responsibility over whom you don't have authority. You can have a positive impact on your manager, as well as your work colleagues, in striving to make changes happen that lead to better outcomes for your team, your organisation and you.

Managing involves:

✔ **Planning the work.** Produce detailed plans and schedules for how and when the team's work is to be done, including breaking down major tasks into simple steps and agreeing deadlines.

✔ **Organising people and other resources.** Assign tasks and responsibilities to team members based on their commitment and capability to do the work, and make best use of the knowledge, skills and expertise in your team. Provide the resources necessary to enable people to do their work.

✔ **Monitoring and controlling the work.** Check that the work is being progressed according to plan to achieve the objectives and results your team is expected to deliver.

✔ **Establishing and using systems and processes.** Establish and use systems and procedures, including the use of key performance indicators (KPIs) to ensure that the work is done effectively and efficiently.

✔ **Reviewing progress.** Conduct reviews to identify problems: make decisions to solve problems and take corrective action to get back on track. Use reviews to continue to find more effective and efficient ways of completing projects and tasks.

These two lists indicate that, generally speaking, effective leadership involves taking a fundamental, long-range perspective to work, and enthusing people to excel whereas good management requires you to be hands-on and focused on the day-to-day running of your group or department.

Getting people to follow you

You have the right to manage the people who work for you simply by having the role of being their manager: your job gives you the authority to ask and expect your staff to do whatever is reasonable to get the work done, providing that you're fair and treat people with respect. You've probably experienced occasions when your staff question what you ask them to do, because their interpretation of what's a reasonable request is different from your interpretation. Here are examples of requests that people may consider to be unreasonable:

- Helping a colleague to complete an urgent task when they're already busy.
- Staying later than normal at the end of the day to complete a task when they've plans to go out with their friends.
- Working closely with a colleague whom they don't get on with to complete a task.

Having the right to manage people doesn't mean that all your staff automatically do what you ask them to even when you're being reasonable. At times, you may need to use your authority to ensure that an important task is completed by the required deadline, but the more competent you become in leading people the less you have to use that authority in such situations. You discover how to develop your skills in leading people in Part II.

Earning the right to lead

Some managers are perceived to abuse their authority by the people who report to them. Most people respond positively to being asked to do a task that's reasonable even if it causes them inconvenience, but people don't generally respond well to being told what to do when they think that they're being:

✔ Belittled.

✔ Made to feel that their needs are ignored.

✔ Patronised.

✔ Treated disrespectfully.

Avoid treating people in any of these ways because they can perceive you as abusing your authority and they're not then willingly doing what you ask them to do.

You choose to lead, but the people who work for you choose whether they want to follow you in the sense that they choose whether they're going to do only an 'okay' job or a great job for you. People choose whether to put in the extra effort often necessary to do a great job – often referred to as *discretionary effort* because they've the discretion as to whether they apply it. Engaged employees do great work.

Earn the right to lead your staff by fully engaging them:

✔ Build confidence through everyone knowing that they can come to you at any time with any problems at all.

✔ Inspire them: talk enthusiastically about why and how their work is important, and the consequences of not doing it well.

✔ Respect how they're different to you, without lowering any standards regarding work or behaviour.

✔ Show a genuine interest in them: their needs, hopes and concerns.

✔ Treat them as equals: don't speak down to them.

✔ Value them for who they are, as well as for what they can do for you.

✔ Work with them rather than doing things to them: ask them for, consider and, if appropriate, use their ideas, views and opinions.

Leading and managing together

I'm sure that your job is demanding and you, like most leaders, find fitting everything into your daily schedule difficult: doing your own work as well as leading and managing the people who report to you. You probably experience dilemmas about whether to focus your attention and time on getting the work done or dealing with staff issues, and whether to spend time managing or investing your time in leading people.

You may end up focusing and spending more time on getting the work done because tasks, unlike staff issues, tend to have deadlines! An example is doing a task yourself rather than delegating it to someone because you think you can complete the task quicker and better than that person, and you don't have time to train someone to do the task before the deadline. Another example is correcting people's mistakes yourself because you think you don't have time to coach them to do the task correctly and hit the deadline.

The reality is that you don't have the luxury of choosing to manage or lead: you need to do both! Yes, you have to deliver results now, but you also have to build commitment and develop the capability of individuals and your team to achieve success in the future: you need to achieve sustainable success.

You have many opportunities to lead and manage people at the same time even though the activities are different (as I describe in the earlier section 'Describing the Key Differences'). For example, during a meeting with your team, you may involve everyone in thinking and deciding how to complete a major task and, in doing so:

- ✔ Enhance how people are working together on solving problems.
- ✔ Enthuse your staff about the importance of the task.
- ✔ Gain their commitment to do a great job.
- ✔ Plan how the task can be completed.
- ✔ Organise who's going to do each sub-task.
- ✔ Reinforce certain standards regarding quality and hitting deadlines.

You need to put more emphasis on managing in some situations and more emphasis on leading people in other situations to achieve success.

Remain conscious at all times of your behaviour and the actions you're taking in leading and managing people, to increase the likelihood of you having the desired effect on your team, and achieving the outcomes you intend.

Although I encourage you to treat every situation as unique, and think about the issues you want to deal with and the outcomes that you want to achieve, you're more likely to adopt the right approach to each situation if you know how to recognise that different situations require a different emphasis on leading and managing in dealing with them:

1. **Divide a piece of paper into three columns as shown in Table 1-4.**

2. **Describe briefly in the first column examples of situations when you need to put more emphasis on** *leading.*

3. **Describe briefly in the second column examples of situations when you need to put more emphasis on** *managing.*

4. **Describe briefly in the last column examples of situations in which you can take opportunities to** *lead and manage at the same time.*

I give a few examples in the first row to help you get started.

Table 1-4	When to Lead, When to Manage and When to Do Both at the Same Time	
Situations in Which I Need to Put More Emphasis on Leading	**Situations in Which I Need to Put More Emphasis on Managing**	**Situations in Which I Can Seize Opportunities to Lead and Manage**
When I need to enthuse people about changes in how we work.	When a job has to be organised quickly to hit an urgent deadline.	During team meetings to plan major tasks and gain commitment from individuals to take on additional responsibilities.

Use your analysis to practise quickly recognising when to put more emphasis on leading or managing in different situations, and adopt the right approach to dealing with each situation.

Continue to reflect on your experiences so that you're constantly refining your leadership and management skills, and make sure that you question yourself about whether you adopted the best approach in different situations.

Chapter 2

Leading 'Inside Out': Knowing Yourself to Become a Better Leader

You don't need to turn yourself inside out to become a better leader, but in order to lead others successfully you do need to know yourself: for example, your preferences, strengths, weaknesses, beliefs and values. To put this idea another way: leading outwards starts with looking inwards. Looking inwards allows you to get to know yourself better, because the better you understand what's important to you and how that affects the way you think and behave, the better you understand why you act and react as you do in different situations. You can then use this 'inside' information to consider how you, as a leader, impact on and affect the people who work with you.

In this chapter, you discover a range of techniques to look inside and at yourself, and how you can learn more from your experiences to better understand yourself and use this knowledge to enhance your leadership ability. You build on this work in Chapter 3, where you discover how to clarify what's important to you – your values – and in Chapter 4, where you develop a sense of purpose that's meaningful to you and others.

Leading Others Starts with Leading Yourself

In the helter-skelter of doing your job, you have to spend time on the things that grab your attention: achieving objectives, hitting deadlines, solving problems with jobs and problems with people!

Focusing all your attention on these areas and other issues means that you may give yourself too little or no attention, with the result that you become less aware of your behaviour and the reasons why you behave the way you do.

 Turning the spotlight on yourself helps to accelerate the process of becoming the leader you aspire to be. Doing so enables you to be more conscious of the following aspects of yourself:

- ✔ Your thoughts and the assumptions you make that affect how you think and interpret information and situations.

- ✔ Your feelings and how they impact on your attitude, especially towards other people.

- ✔ Your behaviour and whether it's intentional or automatic: whether you think things through and act accordingly or whether you act automatically without fully considering the potential impact or effect that your behaviour has on others.

Becoming an authentic leader

Many different descriptions of authentic leadership exist in the management literature. (*Authentic Leadership* by Bill George (Jossey-Bass) gives one example.) In this section I describe the most important aspects of authentic leadership and pose questions for you to reflect on how authentic you are. Initially, however, I need to examine the consequences of being perceived as an inauthentic leader.

Do you recognise any of the following situations in which a leader can be perceived as not being authentic? If you do, what effect did the leader have on you and your desire to follow that person?

- ✔ The leader says, 'It's not me who's asking you to make these changes, I'm just the messenger.'

- ✔ The leader abdicates responsibility by doing nothing when she can see tension or conflict between members of the team.

- ✔ The leader praises a member of the team for doing a task badly.

- ✔ The leader is perceived as having 'slopy shoulders': that is, she avoids taking responsibility for something that goes wrong.

- ✔ The leader was prepared to criticise some people but not others for the same errors.

- ✔ The leader wasn't prepared to tackle people who were known to be prickly, temperamental or unpleasant.

If you ever catch yourself doing any of the above behaviour, be aware of the potential consequences that such actions can have for you and your colleagues!

So what are the consequences of you being perceived by your staff or other work colleagues as inauthentic?

Your staff or work colleagues question themselves or doubt whether they should, or worse decide not to, follow you when they perceive you as not being authentic. In practice, they may comply with what you expect of them, but you don't get their full commitment.

Authentic leaders:

- ✔ **Know themselves.** They invest time questioning and clarifying who they are and what's important to them: that is, their values. Develop your own self-knowledge so that you can be authentic by working through questions such as:

  - What's important to me?

  - What are my values?

  - What makes me happy and what do I get upset about?

✔ **Are genuine.** Total alignment exists between who the leader is and what she does, so that followers see the leader's 'true self'. Authentic leaders also have a genuine, rather than superficial, interest in others: their need to do meaningful work, and their hopes and concerns. Challenge yourself about whether you're always genuine by asking questions such as:

- Do I always behave in line with my values even though I may choose to modify my behaviour according to the needs of others or the situation?

- Do I really value people for who they are as well as what they can do for me?

- Do I acknowledge my weaknesses as well as my strengths in working with others?

✔ **Are open and honest.** Authentic leaders have the courage of their convictions and say what they think even if that means standing out from the crowd: they tell the truth. They're also open or receptive to others' views and opinions.

Do you ever catch yourself holding back and keeping your views to yourself in meetings, especially if you:

- Disagree with proposed decisions and actions?

- Consider the behaviour of a colleague to be unacceptable?

If you do notice yourself behaving this way, ask yourself the following questions:

- Why am I not expressing my thoughts and opinions?

- What do I think is going to happen to me if I do share my views, and why do I think this way?

Most people are uncomfortable about expressing their views in a meeting if they think they're going to be embarrassed or may embarrass others by stating their opinion. (Refer to the later section 'Being comfortable with being uncomfortable' to discover a simple technique to help you to face up to and address difficult situations by becoming more comfortable being uncomfortable.)

Answering the above questions allows you to gain further insights into, and build upon, your leadership and management strengths and development needs (check out Chapter 1 for help with these aspects). Use leadership learning plans as described in the later section 'Achieving more by learning quickly' to plan how you're going to work on your leadership development needs.

Looking through the Johari Window

As well as looking at and inside yourself, I also encourage you to seek feedback from other people to increase your self-knowledge. To show the extent to which people see (or crucially don't see) themselves effectively, I use the Johari Window – developed by Joseph Lufts and Harry Ingrams and shown in Figure 2-1. This model shows in the first column what you do know about yourself and in the second what you don't know about yourself, and helps to explain just why seeking feedback from others is so important. I refer to each quadrant in Figure 2-1 as panes in a window.

	Known to self	Not known to self
Known to others	Open	Blind
Not known to others	Hidden	Unknown

Figure 2-1: The views through the Johari Window.

'Open' pane

Like everyone, I'm sure that you're comfortable sharing a certain amount of self-knowledge or information about yourself with other people. Figure 2-1's 'open' pane represents this type of knowledge – which is known to both yourself and others – for example:

✔ Describing the work you do and the jobs you've held.

✔ Talking about your personal life, including your family details, interests, hobbies and so on.

✔ Revealing your preferences, likes and dislikes.

'Hidden' pane

In contrast to the 'open' knowledge, some information you may deliberately choose not to share with (or may indeed deliberately hide from) others (the 'hidden' pane in Figure 2-1). Choosing not to share such information is equivalent to painting over this pane so as to obscure from people what you prefer to keep to yourself. This knowledge may include, for example, things you've done in the past about which you're embarrassed.

'Blind' pane

The first two panes – 'open' and 'hidden' – comprise knowledge about yourself that you know and then choose to share with others or hide. In contrast, the other two panes consist of knowledge that you don't know about yourself.

Other people may well hold different views about you than you hold of yourself. For example, you may see yourself as a strong assertive character while others perceive your behaviour as being aggressive. If people choose not to share their views about you with you – probably bits of your behaviour or attitude that they'd like you to change – then what's apparent to them remains 'blind' to you (the 'blind' pane in Figure 2-1). This pane is equivalent to one-way glass: people see you but you don't see yourself. Because you don't notice the effect your behaviour has on other people (but that effect is apparent to them), this crucial pane is the one that you can illuminate by getting feedback from others. (Refer to the later sidebar 'I can't change if nobody tells me!' for an example of me giving feedback to a senior manager about the effect his behaviour was having on his staff.)

Many people don't share their views about you with you, however, if they think that you're going to be embarrassed or threatened by what they say, or they themselves feel embarrassed or threatened by sharing their views with you. Despite the potential awkwardness, try to seek out the views of others so you can gain insights into the effect you're having on your staff and other work colleagues. This process is the basis of 360-degree feedback used in leadership development programmes in many organisations, when feedback is sought from people who work for and with the leader about the extent to which the leader is considered to have certain competencies that the organisation considers to be important.

I can't change if nobody tells me!

Pete was a Technical Director in a company he'd started with a partner. The company had grown over several years and now employed almost 100 people, many as engineers. As Technical Director, Pete had the right to check on all the designs for the engineering projects being worked on and took on this responsibility with gusto, almost as if he were holding court standing at a big table in the centre of the open-plan design office. Engineers brought their designs to the table and gave updates on how their projects were progressing.

Being a great engineer, Pete quickly spotted flaws or identified improvements in the designs. He had a booming voice, and everyone in the design office knew about the flaws and improvements required in each design as well as the relevant project engineer. Consequently, engineers weren't enthusiastic about having project reviews!

When, as part of a leadership development programme, I explained to him the effects of his behaviour on the engineers, it was immediately clear that nobody had ever mentioned this problem to Pete: he was totally unaware of the impact his project reviews had on engineers. He commented: 'I wish someone had pointed this out to me years ago and I could've done something about my behaviour!'.

'Unknown' pane

Certain aspects of yourself exist that no one has yet discovered or seen. The information, under the 'unknown' pane in Figure 2-1, contains those aspects that neither you or other people know at the moment, and this pane indicates that you're on a lifelong journey of discovery. You can discover more about yourself through having new experiences and assessing how well you cope with them.

You can accelerate developing into the leader you want to be by actively seeking feedback from the people who report to, and work with, you about the effect you have on them and how they perceive you. Play to your strengths and work on your weaknesses. By seeking and using the views of your colleagues to improve yourself, you set a great example and are encouraging others to do the same.

Enhance your self-knowledge by asking people who report to you and other work colleagues for their views about you: that is, how they perceive you. Then compare and contrast how their views 'fit' with your own views of yourself.

As everyone is different, two people are never going to see things exactly the same. You can test this fact by completing the following short exercise and, at the same time, practise your skills in seeking and using feedback from others:

1. **Select an event or experience that you shared with a friend or colleague.** It may be a television programme or film you both saw, a speech you both heard or even a meeting you both attended.

2. **Ask your friend or colleague to describe her interpretation of the event and then share your interpretation.** Seek the other person's perspective *before* you share your own view.

3. **Give your friend or colleague your full attention while she's talking and suspend judgement while listening.** Don't interrupt or make decisions about whether you agree or disagree with the other person's interpretation. I'm not suggesting that you let go of your views or beliefs about the event, only that you stay open to another interpretation. When you become open to other interpretations, you sometimes find that those interpretations are more meaningful than your own: you discover how to be open to changing some of your views, assumptions or beliefs because you're questioning them.

Now apply this approach to seeking feedback about yourself:

1. **Seek the views of a colleague about you and notice any differences between how that person perceives you and how you see yourself.**

2. **Notice your own reactions to what the person says, because noticing differences in viewpoints can sometimes surprise or even shock you.** Make a mental note of you reactions or write them down.

3. **Question yourself about why you reacted that way.** For example, if someone's view surprises you, you must have been assuming that something else was

true. If something someone says shocks you, you must believe something contrary to what the person is saying. Being surprised or shocked by another person's view or belief can expose and help you clarify your own views, assumptions and beliefs.

Questioning yourself about why you hold particular assumptions and beliefs can also lead you to change them.

Developing Self-Confidence

Most leaders have doubts about their ability to succeed at one time or another, especially when faced with difficult situations. Developing your self-confidence is an essential part of you becoming a great leader because:

✔ You're willing to step outside of your comfort zone (the next section 'Being comfortable with being uncomfortable' helps you to clarify those situations that are inside and outside your comfort zone).

✔ You're more likely to think through and be prepared for the risks involved in stepping outside of your comfort zone.

✔ You're enhancing your leadership skills through confronting and dealing with difficult situations and problems that you've never previously encountered.

You can work on building your self-confidence by:

✔ **Acknowledging that nobody is perfect, including you.** Try to be the best you can be without beating yourself up for not being perfect.

✔ **Catching yourself being successful.** You probably tend to notice problems and failures more than successes, and you can boost your confidence by actively looking for and recognising your successes. Praise yourself for doing a task well, although you may want to do so quietly to avoid receiving strange looks from your colleagues!

✔ **Appreciating that 'good enough' is okay when, for example, you're working on completing certain tasks.** Yes, you want to do the best job you can because it reflects on you, but recognising when a task is good enough (in that it meets the requirements) helps you to recognise that sometimes your work, and therefore you, are good enough.

✔ **Sharing the problems and difficult situations you experience with someone you trust and respect.** You often gain insights into what to do just by talking through problems, and doing so can enhance your confidence to tackle effectively the problems you're experiencing.

Becoming comfortable with being uncomfortable

Most people prefer to be comfortable rather than uncomfortable. For example, when you arrive home after work you may well sink into your most comfortable chair or sofa instead of settling for a seat in which you can't totally relax.

Similarly, in the work environment, most people prefer to remain in their comfort zone. *Comfort zone* is a term used widely in personal and leadership development to describe the state in which a person feels safe or at ease: a mental and emotional state I also describe as 'comfortable'. When you're operating in your comfort zone, you're at ease with yourself. You're in a situation or doing an activity that allows you to work within the limits of your perceived skills and abilities: or put another way, you feel comfortable because you're confident that you can do the activity well or deal with the situation.

Staying in your comfort zone is therefore risk-free because you don't expose yourself to potential failure. But developing your leadership skills can never be risk-free, otherwise you never discover how to handle potentially difficult problems.

Instead, you need to face up to and deal with difficult situations, and therefore you can expect to feel uncomfortable in your new leadership role. Unfortunately, too many new leaders don't accept this reality and refuse to face up to difficult problems or people. Instead, they delay dealing with them or even ignore them, which often means that the problem gets bigger as the work situation deteriorates.

Figure 2-2 gives a couple of examples of the types of situations that may be outside your comfort zone. Add your own dilemmas to the diagram and create a picture of your own, personal comfort zone. Write those dilemmas that are just outside your comfort zone closer to the centre circle, and those that you feel involve more risk farther away from the centre. Also, include a few examples of situations that are inside your comfort zone to ensure that you also recognise your strengths.

Figure 2-2: What's inside and outside your comfort zone?

Facing up to problems and exposing yourself to new potentially difficult situations involves stepping outside of your comfort zone and being uncomfortable. In this way you can discover how to become 'comfortable being uncomfortable' and build the confidence that you can cope with new situations and be successful in dealing with them.

Finding out how to be comfortable being uncomfortable also enables you to stretch yourself and develop your leadership abilities. Working through how to deal with difficult situations and problems enables you to develop your problem-solving and decision-making skills, convey the standards of work and behaviour you expect from others, practise your skills in working effectively with difficult people and so on. Developing your leadership abilities also enhances your self-confidence in handling new situations, which in turn enables you to expand your comfort zone because you then feel more at ease when you're exposed to new difficult situations in the future.

To encourage you to face up to and address a difficult situation or put yourself into a new situation that involves a degree of risk, consider and answer the following questions:

- ✔ **What's the worst possible outcome if I address this situation?**
- ✔ **What's the best possible outcome of this situation?**
- ✔ **What's the outcome that's in the middle of these two outcomes?**
- ✔ **What's the probability of each of these outcomes happening?**

Answering these questions may well confirm that you're over-estimating the seriousness of the problem or the likelihood or it occurring. New leaders often don't face up to situations because they're concerned about the outcome, without objectively assessing what the outcome may be: they're concerned about the worst outcome even though the probability of it happening is miniscule!

One of the most common outcomes that people tell me they're concerned about is feeling embarrassed due to not dealing with a difficult situation very well. When I enquire how long they feel embarrassed, most people say a few hours or a day or two at most. In fact, the chances of you dealing so badly with a situation that you're left with an emotional scar is extremely rare. Clarifying the best and middle outcomes can encourage you to address the difficult situation because you place equal emphasis on the positives as well as the negatives. Recognising and appreciating the benefits of dealing with the situation can also prompt you to act.

Being your best critic

One way of building your self-confidence is to take responsibility for solving problems or handling difficult situations that you come across, including those to which you contribute or cause. You can continually enhance your skills in solving problems and handling difficulties by learning from your experiences.

Being your own best critic involves adopting a 'critical friend' approach in which you constructively critique – rather than destructively criticise – yourself. Focus on questioning your motives, attitude and behaviour in leading people, because you're intent on enhancing your self-knowledge and leadership ability. You're on a journey of discovery, trying to find out how to prevent problems and difficult situations occurring or reoccurring.

Being your own best critic requires you to do the following:

✔ Construct a positive 'I want to (learn to) be better' mentality to encourage yourself to examine and improve on what you do.

  To recognise the value of continuously working on your development, take a few minutes to think about and note how you've developed as a leader over the last year, and how the changes you've made in how you lead have benefitted you and the people who report to you. (Discover the different language used by people with positive and negative attitudes towards facing up to and handling difficult situations in the next section 'Learning from adversity'.)

✔ Be objective in constructively critiquing the action you took and why you took it in dealing with recent problems and difficult situations. Use facts and evidence about each situation wherever you can when conducting your analysis.

✔ Build progressively on your leadership strengths by working on the personal insights you gain from constructively critiquing yourself. Note the progress you're making and tell yourself 'well done [use your name here]' for solving the problems you encounter.

Always use your own name when giving yourself praise for doing a job well, because the praise is more powerful as personal recognition and reinforcement when your hear your name attached to the praise. For the same reason, always use the person's name when you're praising a colleague.

Find out more about learning from your experiences in the later section 'Discovering How to Lead from Your Experiences'.

Learning from adversity

In the early stages of my career, an occupational psychologist once described me as a 'maximiser', because I was always keen to explore the dilemmas I was experiencing in leading people and find out as much as possible about how to handle 'people problems' – or perhaps I should say 'problem people'. I'm certainly not suggesting that you create or cause problems just so that you can learn from them, but I do encourage you to see problems, difficult situations and dilemmas as opportunities to find out how to handle them effectively.

Adopt a positive rather than negative attitude towards difficult situations so that you can learn as much as you can from adversity.

The following short exercise helps to see whether you need to work on developing a more positive attitude:

1. **Take a few minutes to think about and note down the words or phrases that typically come into your mind when you're faced with a problem or difficult situation.**

2. **Compare your notes with the words in the first column of Table 2-1.** If most of the words or phrases in your list are the same as or similar, you probably don't like, or try to avoid, adversity. Try using the equivalent words or phrase in the second column when you're faced with adversity, because using these words and phrases give you a more positive attitude to dealing with adversity. You're then more likely to discover how to deal with such adversities effectively.

3. **Compare your notes with the words in the second column of Table 2-1.** If most of the words or phrases in your list are the same as or similar, you're probably willing to tackle adversity. Give yourself a pat on the back and keep up the good work!

Table 2-1	Negative and Positive Language
Negative Language	*Positive Language*
I can't (handle this).	I can (handle this).
I should/need to (do. . .)	I will (do. . .)
It's not my fault (that this problem exists).	I'm responsible (for solving this problem).
It's a problem.	It's an opportunity.
I don't know how (to solve this. . .)	I will find out how (to. . .)
We will do it but it will be difficult.	We will do it even though it will be difficult.

Discovering How to Lead from Your Experiences

Taking on board lessons from your experiences is a very powerful form of learning, because you remember your successful actions – the ones that achieve your aims – and discard or change your behaviour when you fail to achieve your aims. This process is the basis of learning through 'trial and error'. Unfortunately, 'trial and error' can be quite a slow and painful process because you:

✔ Tend mainly to notice and learn from significant events: those that go really well or very badly.

✔ Have to keep having new experiences from which you can learn and develop your leadership ability.

In this section, I show you how to accelerate and increase learning from your experiences.

Achieving more by learning quickly

You can speed up learning from your experiences by adopting a more structured approach called the *learning cycle*, a technique made famous by experiential learning and organisational behaviour expert David Kolb. The learning cycle contains four steps or activities:

1. **Acting:** Taking action and appreciating the immediate impact or effect the experience has on your knowledge, understanding and skills as a leader.

2. **Reflecting:** Reflecting back on the experience after the event to clarify and identify the main or significant actions you took, and possible causes or consequences of those actions.

3. **Theorising:** Acquiring insights and learning lessons about what works and doesn't work from the links you make between actions and outcomes.

4. **Planning:** Making plans to apply the lessons you've learnt.

The cycle then starts again by you taking the action you plan to take, reflecting on it and so on. Making this cycle part of your everyday practice enables you to accelerate developing your leadership skills through a more structured and thorough approach than simple trial and error, enabling you to use these skills to achieve more in leading your team.

The following example demonstrates how the learning cycle can be applied to finding out how to ride a bicycle. Assume that you're only a few years old and have just had the stabilisers removed from your bicycle. You've come to a steep descent and are peddling quite hard. Your speed increases more than you expect and your exhilaration at going fast suddenly turns to fear for your safety:

You take *action* that causes the bike to stop suddenly and tip forward throwing you over the handlebars.

By *reflecting* on the experience, you identify that you pulled the front brake on immediately before the bike tipped forward.

By *theorising*, you learn the lesson that pulling the front brake on when you're going fast causes the bike to tip over, and you learn to pull the rear brake to stop the bike safely without you being thrown over the handlebars.

You *plan* to use this newly acquired knowledge about riding a bike as soon as you get back on your bike.

Use leadership learning plans as part of your structured approach to planning how you're going to work on your leadership and management development needs. Table 2-2 provides a structure of a leadership learning plan and contains an example of how to use the plan.

In Chapter 1, I present exercises on your expectations of leaders and managers. If you haven't already, complete these exercises and use the leadership and management development needs you identified to complete the following exercise:

1. **Complete a plan for each leadership development need or objective by answering the questions at the top of each column.**

2. **Use the learning plans you complete to develop your leadership skills as quickly as you can, and then to assess how well you're applying the knowledge and skills you acquire in the workplace to improve your own and others' performance and behaviour.**

Table 2-2   Example of a Leadership Learning Plan

Description of my Learning Objective	How I'm Going to Achieve my Learning Objective	My Deadline for Achieving This Objective	How I'm going to Measure my Success in Achieving my Learning Objective?
To be skilled in constructively challenging unacceptable behaviour and performance	Attend an influencing skills workshop that meets my learning objective	By 30 June 2011	I'll be confident and effective in resolving inter-personal problems.
	Practise using the knowledge and skills I acquire in working with my colleagues	By 30 September 2011	The performance and behaviour of each individual I work with will meet the standards I expect/require of them.

Harnessing the power of reflection

Your working day is probably the same as that of most leaders: hectic! Busy, busy, busy, with so much on your mind, as you strive to get through all your work, hit your deadlines and deal with the crises that keep cropping up. You don't have time to be still, and you may well ask why would you want to be still when you've so much to do? Because being still and calming your mind is necessary for you to be reflective.

Perhaps an analogy may help. Cars and other vehicles have reflectors on the back of them. The purpose of these reflectors is to catch light from the headlights of other vehicles and reflect the light back so that the vehicle can be seen. Reflecting involves you shining a light into your past experiences so that you can see into, and make sense of, them.

Reflecting enables you to notice and see things that may not have been immediately apparent to you when the experience occurred. You gain insights into each experience by making connections between, for example, the actions and reactions of yourself and others involved in the event. These connections enable you to identify the causes and effects of these actions and reactions.

Reflecting is an important enough activity for you to spend time doing it.

Most leaders find that reflecting on and learning as much as they can from their experiences is difficult because:

- ✔ They've so much to do and feel under pressure to complete their workload and hit deadlines.
- ✔ They've no pressing deadline for the activity of reflecting and so it can keep dropping towards the bottom of the 'to do' list.
- ✔ They don't appreciate the value of reflecting.
- ✔ They aren't skilled in reflecting.

Make time every day to reflect on and learn from your experiences of the day and get into the habit of asking yourself questions such as the following:

- ✔ What did I do well today?
- ✔ What could I have done better?
- ✔ What action(s) did I take that helped me and/or my team succeed?
- ✔ What action(s) should I have taken, and what were the outcomes or consequences of my inactivity?
- ✔ What would I do differently if I were in a similar situation again?
- ✔ What have I discovered from reflecting on today's experiences?

Developing skills in reflecting

Although some people are naturally more reflective than others, you can develop your skills in reflecting on and learning from your experiences.

Become a more skilful reflector by starting to do the following activities:

- ✔ **Being more self-aware.** Practise noticing what you do in, for example, meetings. Do you tend to speak up more or less than your colleagues? Reflection involves looking back into your experiences, and so you may want to conduct a review of your contribution to a meeting after the meeting finishes or even during the meeting itself. However, be careful to avoid becoming so engrossed in yourself that you miss important points being made by your colleagues on the topics being discussed.

- ✔ **Questioning yourself.** As you become more aware of your behaviour in meetings and other situations, question yourself about the reasons for behaving the way you do in these situations. Questioning yourself about the assumptions or beliefs that cause you to behave as you do provides valuable insights into whether your assumptions and beliefs are valid . . . or whether you need to change some of them!

✔ **Noticing what's significant.** People who are skilled in reflecting on situations or events are able to pick out the actions that were significant in contributing to or causing or affecting the outcomes of each situation. Taking meetings as an example, outcomes may include such things as decisions made, the commitment of individuals to take the actions that were agreed, the attitude of attendees towards the value of the meeting and much more.

Practise your skills in noticing what's significant by observing and noting down how people act and react to each other and what's said in meetings. Examine your notes after the meeting to identify connections or 'causes and effects' between the points you note, and use your analysis to enhance your understanding of how individuals are influencing and being influenced by the arguments, actions and behaviour of people at the meeting.

The next time you go along to a professional gathering or event, actively listen to what others from different industries to your own say. See whether you can include one or two of their ideas in your own situation.

✔ **Calming your mind.** Being reflective doesn't involve thinking about and planning what tasks you're going to do next: reflecting is a backward-looking and not a forward-looking activity. When you're busy, reflecting can be difficult because your mind is full of things you have to do, and so initially you need to practise clearing or calming your mind as follows:

Find a calm or quiet place in which you can be reflective. Choose a place where your mind won't be distracted: perhaps a quiet office, a quiet corner of a café, your journey home on the train or somewhere similar.

Relax your body by settling into a comfortable chair. Take a few deep breaths and feel any tension leave your body as you slowly exhale. Let go of irrelevant thoughts by refocusing on the situation or event on which you're reflecting. Writing brief notes about the situation and focusing your thoughts on your notes help you to stay focused. (*Mindfulness For Dummies* by Shamash Alidina (Wiley) has a wealth of advice for calming your mind.)

Using leadership learning logs

The main value in you keeping a leadership learning log is for you to optimise your learning by critically reflecting on your experiences, and through this activity improve your reflection skills. Table 2-3 provides the structure for critically reflecting on your experiences, and in the second and third rows I provide an example (of attending a meeting) to show how you can complete it.

Table 2-3	Example of a Leadership Learning Log	
Describe the Experience	*Reflect on and Review the Experience*	*Learning and Application*
Give a brief account of what happened, describe your behaviour, thoughts and feelings, and then the behaviour of others involved in the situation.	What was especially significant about what happened? How do you now feel about the experience? What conclusions can you draw from your experiences, including any possible causes and/ or potential consequences with regard to what happened?	What have you found out from reflecting on your experiences? What insights or interpretations have you gained? For example, confirmation of something you already know, a new way of looking at an old issue or something new that you didn't know before. How, and when, do you plan to use this knowledge and/or skills?

continued

Table 2-3 *(continued)*

Describe the Experience	Reflect on and Review the Experience	Learning and Application
I attended one of my occasional meetings with senior managers regarding a potential new book. I had several good ideas but didn't speak up because I wasn't confident that my ideas were good enough. Other people then made proposals similar to my own, which were accepted. I felt annoyed with myself for not speaking up.	I now recognise that I tend to hold back too much in meetings until I become familiar with the people. Senior managers probably see me as not being creative, which is untrue. I don't get recognition and may be overlooked for future promotions. I'm still a bit annoyed with myself, but am using this feeling to prompt myself to act differently in future meetings.	I'm going to practise speaking up more in all types of meetings I attend. I recognise that I may sometimes feel embarrassed when my ideas and opinions aren't accepted, but I'm telling myself that I can cope with any criticism. I'll become more confident as people accept my good ideas, and will overcome feeling embarrassed through more exposure to my views being questioned.

Finding and working with your own coach

Finding and working with your own coach enables you to accelerate becoming the leader you aspire to be. Use your coach as follows:

✔ As a sounding board to provide independent and objective feedback to you about your ideas and plans.

✔ To examine significant events you want to explore, and offer alternative views, perspectives and interpretations to help you to better understand them.

✔ As a source of moral support to enable you to resolve difficult dilemmas.

✔ To support and challenge you in examining your intentions, motives and appropriateness of your behaviour in a wide range of work situations.

As your coach, seek someone you admire for their professional expertise and achievements and/or someone you can trust and respect: the latter two attributes are essential because you want to be open with the person and sometimes explore sensitive, confidential, personal or commercial issues.

Look for someone who:

✔ Respects and maintains the confidentiality of your conversations.

✔ Is a good listener and hears you out without interrupting.

✔ Asks searching questions to prompt you to question your own thoughts and decisions.

✔ Provides honest and independent feedback to you.

Pluck up the courage to ask the person you most admire to be your coach regardless of her position in your organisation. Most senior managers appreciate being asked to perform this role because you're paying them a compliment by letting them know that you value them. If the person agrees to be your coach, you need to clarify the following items:

✔ Their role as your coach.

✔ The expectations you have of each other.

✔ How frequently you're going to meet.

✔ How you plan to review jointly whether the relationship is working for both of you.

✔ How you'll know when to end the coaching relationship, and how you're going to end it.

Good luck in your search!

Chapter 3

Singing Your Leadership Song: Being in Tune with Your Values

. . . .

In This Chapter

▶ Knowing when you're out of tune with your values

▶ Appreciating the value of your values

▶ Getting into tune with others

. . . .

*U*nlike me you may have a great singing voice, and yet sometimes when you sing you're going to be out of tune! When this situation happens, your singing talent is wasted because people don't want to listen to you. Being a great leader is sometimes similar to being a great singer: you can have all the skills required for leading effectively, but your colleagues can choose not to follow you when they think that you're not being authentic. In other words, you appear to be out of tune with yourself!

In Chapter 2, I demonstrate the negative consequences when the people who report to you perceive you as being inauthentic: they begin to question themselves and whether they should follow you, and may even decide not to do so. They may comply superficially with what you expect of them, but they don't give you their full commitment.

Chapter 2 also describes two of the key attributes of authentic leaders: they know themselves and they're genuine. In other words, they know what's important to them – they know their values – and their actions and behaviour are always aligned or congruent with those values.

In this chapter you discover how to recognise when you're out of tune with your core values and how to compose your own tune: that is, how to communicate your values to the people who work for you through your words and actions.

Recognising When You're Out of Tune

You may think that you have to know what being 'in tune' means before you can recognise when you're out of tune, but in fact that isn't always the case. Sometimes you just don't feel right about whether or how you need to address a situation. Or when you're aware that you could have handled a situation better, you continue to feel uneasy or uncomfortable about what you should have done or, indeed, did do.

Occasionally, this unease or discomfort can exist for weeks or months or even longer, perhaps not continually but the sensation keeps coming back. You can feel that something is 'gnawing away at you' and you can't put your finger on the problem.

Invest time in finding out what's causing your discomfort. If the sensation keeps returning, it may be a symptom of you being out of tune with yourself regarding something that's important to you: it may even be about something as fundamental as what you want to do or achieve in your life!

Acknowledging when 'it just doesn't feel right'

My personal story in the sidebar 'What's wrong with me?' shows that acknowledging when you just don't feel right is certainly worthwhile. The cause of your discomfort doesn't have to be as profound or go on as long as mine did: it can be as simple as you not behaving in accord with one of your core values for a time. (I describe the importance of core values in the later section 'Questioning what underpins your leadership').

What's wrong with me?

I share this personal story to explain what I mean about feeling vaguely uneasy. When I was in my late 20s, I was interested in starting my own business. I can recall having conversations with people who ran their own companies about how to start my own business, but having two young children and a hefty mortgage I got on with building my career.

When I was in my early 30s, I became more aware of being upset in certain situations. Those situations tended to be times when I wasn't busy. When I was at work I was focused on the jobs I had to do and the deadlines I had to hit, but when I was at home and my mind wasn't so occupied with tasks and deadlines I became irritable. My wife noticed the change in my behaviour and mentioned it to me.

I knew something wasn't right but I was unable to put my finger on it. We talked about various aspects of our life, but concluded that the unease wasn't about any of the typical aspects of family life. Eventually, I sat down and analysed my life by asking myself and answering simple but difficult-to-answer questions such as:

- ✔ When have I been happy and what were the reasons?

- ✔ When have I been sad and what were the reasons?

- ✔ What do I enjoy doing?

- ✔ What do I dislike doing?

From this analysis, which took me a few months to complete, I distilled five words that were important to me: achievement, variety, change, helping (people) and management. Through this long process of questioning myself, I realised that I was out of tune because I wasn't working for myself doing what I really wanted to do, and I was becoming more frustrated because I wasn't working towards making this happen. I decided then to take voluntary severance from the organisation I worked for and started to build a career working for myself based on the five words that were important to me.

I encourage you to notice and acknowledge any persistent feelings or sensations that something feels wrong to you for the following reasons:

- ✔ When something is causing you to feel uneasy, you're likely to carry that emotion and the associated behaviour into working with your colleagues or being with your family and friends. You may upset others even though that's not your intention. Working on clarifying and

> resolving whatever's upsetting you so that you're more 'in tune' with yourself and 'feel right' is necessary for you to behave appropriately when you're around colleagues, family and friends.

✔ When you experience a sense of something not being right, that feeling can keep grabbing your attention. Staying focused can become difficult and you may even be, or appear to others to be, preoccupied. Being in such a state not only wastes your time, but also makes you less productive than you can be.

Act on, rather than ignore, any feelings or sensations of discomfort that persist over a period of time; they're probably symptoms of something important to you, perhaps that one of your core values isn't being fulfilled.

Questioning what underpins your leadership

The values that are important to you have mainly evolved from the following:

✔ Your DNA: your personal make-up (not the stuff you may put on your face!).

✔ Your upbringing: the way your parents or guardians brought you up.

✔ Your life experiences: critical, perhaps life-changing, events and how you interpret them.

The exercise in Chapter 1 about working through your own experiences of leaders and managers helps you to gain insights into the values and associated behaviours that are important to you, and about how you prefer to treat, and be treated by, people.

Your values are descriptions of what is important to you or what you value, but not in a material sense. Some of your values are core values because they're the most important ones to you.

Your values, especially your core values, underpin your approach to leadership because they:

✔ **Have a significant bearing on what you do and how you behave.** For example, if you value being trusted and trust people to get on with their work you're likely to give them more autonomy. But if you believe that people can't be trusted, no doubt you check up on and monitor them closely.

✔ **Guide how you evaluate people and events.** For example, you're more likely to get on well with people who have the same or similar values as you. You may also react strongly towards people who behave in ways that conflict with or undermine your core values.

Like most people, you may well spend little time thinking about what's important to you.

Invest time in clarifying your values, because when you're clear about them you can use them:

✔ To establish principles or reference points when making decisions about how you lead and manage people

✔ To set standards for many aspects of work for yourself and the people who report to you

✔ To resolve dilemmas about how to handle difficult situations and people

✔ To ensure that you act fairly and consistently in working with people who report to, and work with, you

You discover how to clarify the values that are important to you in the later section 'Working out what's important to you'.

Composing Your Own Leadership Tune

You discover in the previous section 'Questioning what underpins your leadership' that your values are the foundation of your approach to leadership, because they've a significant bearing on what you do and how you behave, as well as how you evaluate people and events.

In this section you discover a few techniques to clarify your values and communicate them to your work colleagues.

Investing time in clarifying your values is equivalent to you composing your leadership tune, because being clear about your values and behaving in ways that are in accord with and promote them enables you to be 'in tune' with yourself. When you're 'on song' in this way, your staff recognise that you're being authentic: they see that you know your core values and are behaving in ways that fit with them.

Being an authentic leader requires you to show a genuine interest in other people, as well as being true to yourself by behaving in accord with your values. You can't be authentic by focusing on what's important to you while ignoring the needs and values of other people.

Working out what's important to you

When meeting you for the first time, many people ask the following question: 'What do you do for a living?'. This question is fairly easy to answer, but what do you say when someone asks 'Who are you?' or 'What's important to you?'. You may well find these questions more difficult to answer unless you've invested time in getting to know yourself. Take time now to start knowing yourself better by completing the following exercise on clarifying your values:

1. **Take a few minutes to consider the questions at the end of this list.** Identify the ones that seem most relevant or helpful in clarifying what's important to you and copy them into a notebook, leaving plenty of space to answer each question.

2. **Try to come up with and note down any other questions that you think may help you to identify what's important to you.**

3. **Start to answer your questions when you've created a sufficient number.** As a guideline, form a list of between four and seven useful questions: any less than four may cause you to be less thorough than you should be, whereas more than seven can prompt you to start digressing into more general philosophising about your life!

Take as much time as you need to answer your questions: the quality of your thinking in answering each question is much more important than answering it quickly. Leaving the questions partially answered for a time is fine: come back to them when you may want to add to or refine your answers after you've reflected on them.

4. **Pick out recurring or significant words, phrases and themes that run through your answers.**

5. **Use these words, phrases and/or themes to produce a list of your values.** In addition, note one or two behaviours that demonstrate that you're behaving in accord with each of those values.

6. **Record these words, phrases and themes in Table 3-1.** Insert a bullet point for each value so that you can refer to it when you're working on becoming an authentic leader and a great role model (I cover the latter subject in Chapter 8). In the table, I provide one example of a value and two appropriate behaviours.

Here are the questions to select from, to help discover your values:

✔ What's important to me about being a leader and how I lead people?

✔ What are my values, especially my core values?

✔ What's important to me about how I'm treated and how I treat others?

✔ What's important to me about how people work together?

✔ What work topics and issues generate most energy, positive or negative, within me?

✔ What positive impact or difference do I want to make to my organisation and/or my work team?

✔ What would need to happen at work for me to have a real sense of fulfilment?

✔ What topics tend to grab my attention and/or what do I talk about a lot at work?

> ✔ In terms of what is right and wrong, what are my absolute standards?
>
> ✔ What mark do I want to leave on the world, the organisation, and the people around me?
>
> ✔ What would my organisation's values be if I could choose them?

Table 3-1 Values and Behaviours that Demonstrate I'm Behaving in Accord with My Values

My Values	*Appropriate Behaviours*
Respect everyone.	I encourage people to express, and I consider, their ideas and opinions.
	I treat everyone fairly.

Walk your talk! Live your values by behaving in ways that fit with them because doing so is the best way to promote and reinforce them: people who report to you take more notice of what you do than what you say.

Questioning your assumptions

You may assume that you always act in accord with your values, but unfortunately this may not always be the case. For example, you may value treating people with respect and not notice when talking to them about completing a task that you're being curt, because you're anxious and under pressure to hit a deadline.

Instead of simply assuming that you always behave in accord with your values, try the following:

- ✔ Question and challenge yourself about whether you always behave as you intend to behave.

- ✔ Try to notice how you behave in different situations – especially when you're under pressure – and compare your behaviour with the behaviours you listed next to your values in Table 3-1 in the preceding section, 'Working out what's important to you'.

- ✔ Share your values, and how you intend to behave, with the people who report to you: seek feedback from them about whether you always behave as you intend, and how your behaviour affects them.

You may also find yourself assuming that other people place the same importance, or equally value, on what's important to you, or presuming that the way you prefer to work is the same for them. You may be right, but you may also be wrong!

If significant differences exist in the values or the preferred ways of working among the people in your team, including you, you're likely to experience problems in leading them and how well they work together. You can find out how to involve members of your team in clarifying and agreeing the values and behaviours to guide how they work together in Chapter 11.

Singing Your Leadership Song

One of my colleagues tells leaders that they're 'teachers without a voice', meaning that leaders are role models: the people who report to you take notice of and copy what you do. Modelling the behaviours that you want other people to adopt is a powerful way of communicating the values and behaviours that are important to you.

Communicating your values

Whenever possible, use face-to-face communication to convey your values, and the associated behaviours, to the people who report to and work with you.

I'm sure that you're relieved to find out that you don't literally have to do a song and dance act to share your values with your staff! Your words and actions, however, do need to be aligned or congruent with your values for you to be authentic and help reinforce your intended message to your work colleagues.

Using face-to-face communication gets across your important values and the relevant behaviours far better than email or other written forms of communication because:

✔ You're trying to achieve more than just informing your work colleagues about your values: you have to influence them so they appreciate that your values are important to you and how your team works. Face-to-face communication is a more effective means of influencing people than other forms of communication because you can see the effect you're having on your colleagues and act accordingly, such as by expanding on or clarifying certain points.

✔ You're using both sight and hearing, and research indicates that people take in more information through their sight than through just hearing the words.

✔ You can engage your colleagues more effectively in exploring the values and behaviours that you're sharing with them and what they mean in practise for how you all work together.

Face-to-face communications in which you sit around the same table as your colleagues is best, but having a video conference may be necessary if some of your staff are in different locations or even on different continents. Get close to the camera when using video conferencing so that people can clearly see you, especially your face.

Harmonising with others

As the buck stops with you in the sense that you're accountable for ensuring that your team achieve objectives and complete tasks to the right standard by the required deadline, you may think that you've the right to impose your values and behaviours on your staff.

As Chapter 1 describes, generally people don't respond well to being told what to do, especially when they feel they're being treated disrespectfully or made to feel inferior. A simple way to cause people you work with to feel inferior or disrespected is to emphasise your values and ignore the values that are important to them.

Be careful to avoid promoting your values over the values of people you work with especially when the national culture of some of your work colleagues is significantly different to your own national culture.

To help you harmonise your values with a work colleague, perhaps a team member, peer or even your boss, have a meaningful dialogue with him as follows:

1. **Approach your colleague and suggest that you explore what's important to you both in how you work together, with the aim of better understanding each other and improving workflow and productivity.**

2. **Agree to produce separately a list of the values that are important to each of you and note what you expect of each other in working together.** You may need to explain the importance of values by drawing on the content of the earlier section 'Questioning what underpins your leadership'.

3. **Complete your lists before you next meet.**

4. **Take turns during your next meeting to share each of the values and the expectations that you have of each other.** Look for similarities to reinforce how close you are to each other already, and explore differences and the ways they can be reconciled in order to agree how you're going to work more effectively together in the future. Agree when and how you plan jointly to review how well you put the agreements into practice.

5. **Conduct reviews using facts and evidence of how you've worked together – particularly emphasising successes – to build progressively on good practice and strengthen your relationship.** Where evidence emerges that you could work better together, jointly suggest and agree how you're going to make improvements.

For a way to harmonise your values with everyone in your team, complete the relevant exercise in Chapter 11 on creating a set of team values with your staff.

Part II
Leading Yourself

'Before we start on the leadership
training, I hope you're not feeling too nervous.'

In this part . . .

*1*f raising the commitment and optimising the performance of people who work with you is your major interest, then this is the main part for you. In these chapters you find out about the importance of purposeful work, and I explain how you can really engage people so that they want to follow you and do their job to the best of their ability. You discover how you can become an engaging leader and modify your leadership style to suit different situations you experience. You find out how to handle people who aren't performing to your standards, and coach good performers towards exceptional results.

Chapter 4

Developing a Sense of Purpose

. . . .

In This Chapter

▶ Clarifying how you add value to your organisation

▶ Discovering how to be a visionary leader

▶ Becoming more influential

. . . .

*'W*hat's the point?' Have you ever asked this question, or maybe heard a work colleague ask it, about a change being introduced to the way your department, team or you work? Perhaps you've experienced occasions when you and/or your work colleagues think that proposals to change the organisational structure, systems or processes (or perhaps instructions from senior management to follow a particular course of action) are completely pointless!

People like to know the point, or purpose, of their work: you can't expect people to do a job or task to the best of their ability if they don't understand the purpose or reasons for doing so. In this chapter you find out how to create a clear sense of purpose that you can use yourself – and communicate to the people who report to you – to focus everyone's efforts on achieving the objectives and results required of you and your team. You also discover how to increase your sphere of influence to encourage people you don't have authority over – including your boss! – so that they act in a way that helps you and your team to be successful.

Having Clarity of Purpose

Your job description, if you have one, describes your duties and responsibilities, but does it clearly describe the purpose of your job and how you contribute to the success of your organisation? For example, does it describe your priorities or how you measure success in doing your job? Probably not!

Or things may have changed so much since your job description was written that it's now out of date, for example, in changes in systems, procedures and even the tasks that you're asked to do. In addition, most job descriptions include the vague phrase '. . .and anything else that is required to. . .' near the end of the description. A good chance exists that you haven't even looked at your job description for ages! With all these uncertainties in mind, developing clarity of purpose can be difficult, which is where this section can help.

I often use the following scenario to challenge leaders on development programmes about how clearly they understand their role in their organisation. I ask them to assume that I'm the new Chief Executive Officer or Managing Director, and that I'm walking around the Head Office stopping individuals and asking them to tell me in 30 seconds:

> *What's the purpose of your job and how do you add value to this organisation?*

To add a bit of spice I also say that I'm looking to make savings and that I'm going to form my initial opinion about the value of each individual's job on the strength of his answer. When answering the question, people tend to tell me what they do rather than describing the positive impact they have in, or the value they add to, their organisation. How well would you answer this question in 30 seconds?

Be so clear about the purpose of your job and your team that you can concisely describe your and their role to them in 30 seconds or less so that they understand how they contribute to the success of your organisation. (Flip to the later section 'Clarifying how you add value' for how to achieve this aim.)

Avoiding being a busy fool

Have you ever experienced any of the following sensations:

- Feeling like you're on a rocking horse, being furiously active but getting nowhere?

- Feeling like you haven't stopped all day and yet have achieved nothing?

- Feeling like you get sucked into the details of your team's work so often that you can't get on with what you're paid to be doing?

- Feeling like you're running around like a headless chicken?

To really add value to your organisation, you need to avoid becoming one of those busy fools who're less productive than they could be.

You may think that you're being effective and efficient because you're very active, but as the song goes 'it ain't necessarily so'! You may, for example, be spending time on tasks or activities that are less valuable or important than other work that you need to do, or so busy because you're disorganised, with one of the following results:

- You're effective, but not efficient.

- You're efficient, but not effective.

- You're not effective or efficient.

Many of the inexperienced and experienced managers that I've worked with on leadership development programmes misunderstand the terms *effective* and *efficient*:

- Being *effective* means focusing on, and spending time doing and completing, the most valuable or important tasks or activities that you have to do and doing them well: it means doing the right things!

- Being *efficient* means using the minimum time and resources to do a particular task or activity: it means doing things the right way!

To help, I use the four-box grid in Figure 4-1 to explain these terms in simple language. The top-right box is the way towards high effectiveness and efficiency.

	Low ——— Efficient ——— High	
High Effective	Doing the right tasks the wrong way	Doing the right tasks the right way
Low	Doing the wrong tasks the wrong way	Doing the wrong tasks the right way

Figure 4-1: Simple explanation of the terms *effective* and *efficient*.

You can avoid being a busy fool by focusing on being effective and efficient: that is, doing the right things the right way!

Being bold: Leading with conviction

The people who report to you expect you to be a decisive leader: they don't want you to 'sit on the fence'. You may, however, sometimes be indecisive because you're unsure about what to do: being bold and leading with conviction in this situation is risky and potentially foolhardy!

Being clear about the purpose of your job, the objectives and results you have to achieve and your priorities enables you to be bolder than you may normally be because you:

- ✔ Confidently communicate the direction that you and your team have to take, and the necessary objectives, targets and results.

- ✔ Convey the direction, objectives and results in ways that the people who report to you understand so that their work becomes meaningful to them.

- ✔ Are more confident that the decisions you make are leading you towards achieving the purpose of your job and your priorities.

✔ Follow through on your decisions and act with commitment to positively influence people and achieve your objectives.

✔ Can explain to anyone and everyone where value is being added and lost in everything that you do.

Clarifying how you add value

Along with everyone else who has a job, you're in the conversion industry: you take *inputs* and convert them into more valuable *outputs*. That's how you add value to the organisation you work for.

Being in the conversion industry doesn't apply only to manufacturing – where companies convert materials into products – it also applies to every service. For example, every time you eat in a restaurant the employees are using information, knowledge, skills, ingredients, equipment and much more to create a great experience and meal for you. Figure 4-2 provides more examples of inputs and outputs.

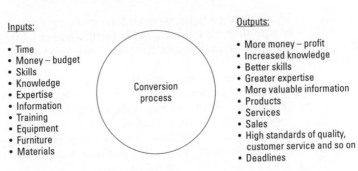

Inputs:

- Time
- Money – budget
- Skills
- Knowledge
- Expertise
- Information
- Training
- Equipment
- Furniture
- Materials

Conversion process

Outputs:

- More money – profit
- Increased knowledge
- Better skills
- Greater expertise
- More valuable information
- Products
- Services
- Sales
- High standards of quality, customer service and so on
- Deadlines

Figure 4-2: The conversion process.

Seeing yourself as being in the conversion process may help you to look at your job from a new perspective. Complete the next exercise to start to clarify how you add value to your organisation by describing the purpose of your job.

Take a look at the lists of inputs and outputs in Figure 4-2:

1. **Tick or circle the words in the first list that describe inputs that you use or consume in carrying out your job.** Add any inputs that you use or consume that aren't on the list, but keep the inputs generic, similar to the points already on the list, instead of dropping in a lot of detail.

2. **Repeat step 1 for the list of outputs.**

3. **Write a sentence that describes the purpose of your job based on some of, if not all, the outputs and inputs you ticked or circled.** I provide two examples below of how the broad purpose of a publisher's job for academic books may be written.

   - **Example 1:** To source, sign and publish the targeted number of books to the required standards and deadlines within budget.

   - **Example 2:** To enhance the knowledge and skills of students, and achieve my profit target by sourcing, signing and publishing academic books.

Which example appeals most to you in terms of the purpose of a publisher's job being most worthwhile or adding most value to the publisher's company, and even to society?

The right answer of course depends on the 'why'! I suggest Example 2 is more appropriate because how value is added – enhancing knowledge and skills, and making a profit – is more explicit in this example than in example 1. So when you write your sentence, make sure that you can support and justify (and if necessary defend) the position that you've taken.

When you're writing a sentence describing the purpose of your job, try to capture the essence or fundamental reason for doing your job: how you add value rather than only 'to earn money'! The purpose of your job needs to capture what's important and worthwhile – and be meaningful rather than meaningless to you and other people when you explain it to them.

The purpose of my job is:

_____

Now work on further clarifying how you add value to your organisation through the work you do by building on the exercise you have just completed.

Before you can be highly productive, you need to have a clear understanding about how what you do helps your organisation to be successful. You need to know what being a 'high performer' in your job means in practice. Completing the following exercise enables you to be clear about what you're expected to achieve and how you can measure your success, which, in turn, helps you to make the right decisions to attain the right results.

Refer to the outputs and inputs you identified and the purpose of your job that you produced when completing the previous exercise and complete the following steps. I give an example of how partially to complete these steps in Table 4-1. (By all means complete these steps in a notebook first while you clarify your thoughts about each step, but also note the outcomes of each step below so that you can use them to focus your efforts and time on achieving the required results. Find out how to do this in the next section, 'Focusing on your key results'.)

1. **List the most important parts of your job.** I suggest that up to five or six most important parts of your job exist: if you're noting more than six, you're probably getting into too much detail:

   A:

   B:

   C:

   D:

   E:

   F:

2. **Write the objectives and/or results that you're expected to achieve in each of the most important parts of your job and how you measure how successful you are in each part.**

Objectives and/or Results I have to Achieve:	How I Measure Success:
A.	
B.	
C.	
D.	
E.	
F.	

Some measures of success may be key success measures, perhaps more commonly known as key performance indicators (KPIs), because those measures or indicators are the most important indicators of performance.

Table 4-1 A Partially Completed Description of a Publisher's Job, and Measuring Success

Most Important Parts of a Publisher's Job:	
A	Publish books to schedule
B	Enhance the knowledge of students in the subject area

Objectives and/or Results a Publisher has to Achieve:	How a Publisher Measures Success:
A. Publish 30 books on schedule in this financial year	Number of books published by the set deadlines
B. Achieve the required uptake and use of books on selected courses	Quality and appearance of subject content Feedback from course leaders and students Recommendations by course leaders Subsequent sales achieved

Share the outcomes of this exercise with your line manager to discuss and agree that you're focusing on the required results, and are working to the right priorities to achieve those results. You may be surprised to find that your manager's views on the purpose, results and/or priorities are slightly (or even significantly) different to your views. Agreeing these items with your manager helps you to work well together by avoiding misunderstandings about what you should be or are doing.

You can only measure whether anything you do is a success or failure against what you set out to achieve.

As the leader of your team, your overall job purpose and objectives are the same as your team's purpose and objectives. Enthusiastically convey the purpose of your team and the objectives and results that you're all aiming for to everyone in your team and to other departments that your team works with and rely upon to succeed. (You can find out how to involve members of your team in clarifying your team's purpose and objectives – if you prefer this alternative approach – in Chapter 11.)

Focusing on your key results

You probably think that you have a lot, perhaps too much, work to complete within the hours stated in your employment contract. Being clear about the objectives and results required to make a valuable contribution to the success of your organisation helps you to be highly productive, but it doesn't guarantee your success. For that, you need a little help from a guy called Vilfredo Pareto.

Pareto was an economist who looked into how land was distributed among people who lived in Italy. Surprise, surprise! Pareto discovered that 20 per cent of the people owned 80 per cent of the land and the basis of the Pareto principle or 80/20 rule was born.

Applying the 80/20 rule to your job means identifying the 20 per cent of the tasks and activities to spend your time on that enable you to be 80 per cent successful in your job. You have to focus on the most valuable tasks and activities: out of all the things you can spend your time doing, you need to decide which tasks and activities are a priority for you to achieve what you need to.

The following descriptions help in understanding how I'm using these terms:

- A *task* is a specific piece of work that you need to do such as one of the steps to complete a project or achieve an objective or result.

- An *activity* is something you do regularly such as holding meetings with your team to discuss how your team is making progress in achieving your team's objectives.

An *urgent* task or activity is one that's very close to the deadline by which it has to be done or completed, whereas a less urgent task is one further away from its deadline.

An urgent task is typically one that has to be done in the next one or two hours or even minutes. For example, completing a document that has to be posted to a client today may be considered to be urgent if the last collection time for the post is within the next one or two hours.

The urgency of a task or activity may change: all you have to do for a task or activity to become more urgent is to not do it and notice how it becomes more urgent as time passes!

An *important* task or activity is one that, by completing, you add a lot of value to your organisation; or put another way, one that contributes significantly to you achieving your objectives and results.

The importance of a task or activity doesn't tend to change unless:

- Senior managers decide to change a company policy or objective, such as to attack a new market, which affects the work you do.

- A change in legislation or another significant external event impacts upon your work responsibilities, such as health and safety legislation.

Figure 4-3 and the following list explain the different combinations of urgency and importance that you may allocate to a task or activity:

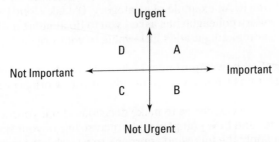

Figure 4-3: Importance and urgency of tasks and activities.

The figure is based on the time management matrix featured in Stephen Covey's Seven Habits of Highly Effective People (Simon and Schuster).

- ✓ **Category 'A' task.** An 'A' task is both urgent and important because completing it significantly contributes to you achieving one of your key objectives and you're close to the deadline for completing it. You may feel under pressure or stress when doing an 'A' task because too little time may be available to do the task as well as you'd like to, and consequences apply if you don't complete it by the required deadline or to the required standard.

- ✓ **Category 'B' task.** A 'B' task is important but not urgent: completing it significantly contributes to you achieving one of your key objectives, but you're not close to the deadline for completing it. You probably feel more relaxed and in control when doing a 'B' task because you've the time you need to do the job well.

- ✓ **Category 'C' task.** A 'C' task is less important than other tasks you have to do and isn't urgent: completing it doesn't significantly contribute to you achieving one of your key objectives and you're not close to the deadline for completing it. You may ask yourself why you're doing a task that you categorise as a 'C' task, which is probably a good question – challenge yourself as to whether it's worthwhile doing it!

✔ **Category 'D' task.** A 'D' task is urgent but less important than other tasks you have to do: completing it doesn't significantly contribute to you achieving one of your key objectives, but you're close to the deadline for completing it. An example of a category 'D' task is one that a work colleague has asked you to do at short notice, but completing it adds little value to your organisation.

Question how important a task or activity is as well as how urgent it is when trying to decide on your work priorities.

Use these categories to make decisions about your work priorities and how you plan and organise use of your time. You can apply the following approach to a workday, week or even a month or longer:

1. **Make a list of all the tasks you have to do in the period you have chosen.**

2. **Go down your list and decide how important and urgent each task is by giving it an 'A', 'B', 'C' or 'D' rating.** If you have given several tasks the same rating, allocate these tasks a secondary rating such as A1, A2, A3 and so on based on the lower the number the higher the priority.

3. **Use the ratings you've given to each task to decide the order in which you're going to do them.**

Bear in mind the following guidelines:

✔ Do more important tasks before less important tasks.

✔ Do 'A' tasks – those that are important and urgent – before 'B' tasks, but make sure that you start 'B' tasks early enough to avoid them becoming 'A' tasks.

✔ Do 'D' tasks if by doing them you stop worrying about them or get a sense of achievement, but do them as quickly as you can.

✔ Leave 'C' tasks alone and only do them if you don't have any 'A', 'B' or 'D' tasks to do.

Spending the right time on the right job

Although deciding on the order in which you're going to do your tasks helps you to 'do the right job' to be effective, it doesn't necessarily make you efficient. (You can find out about the importance of being both effective and efficient in the earlier section 'Avoiding being a busy fool'.) To be efficient, you have to spend the right time on each task: the minimum time required to do the job well.

Use the following techniques to spend the minimum time on each task or activity you have to do to do it well:

- Question yourself whether the job really needs to be done to the standard to which you normally do it. Can you do the job in less time and it still be good enough or 'fit for purpose'?

- Ask yourself, and others, 'What would happen if I didn't do this job?'. Your manager or colleagues may ask you to do extra tasks such as provide additional monthly information or reports to them, but never tell you that they don't need you to do them anymore.

- When you're estimating how long a big job or project may take to complete, break the project down into steps and estimate how long each step is going to take. Then add up the time for each step to produce a more accurate estimate for completing the whole project.

Becoming a Visionary Leader

Many visionary leaders have captured the attention and admiration of the public, and influenced the direction, thinking and behaviour of a large group, society and even a nation. Martin Luther King, Jr. is one of my favourites: I get a tingling sensation every time I hear a recording of his 'I Have a Dream' speech that he gave in 1963.

You don't have to be able to capture the attention of society, but you do have to capture the attention of, and positively influence, the people who report to you if you want them to do a great job for you . . . and being a visionary leader may help you to achieve this aim. I explain how to come up with your vision in the later section 'Creating your own vision', but I introduce being a visionary leader by briefly covering a common process used in many organisations for influencing employees to contribute to the organisation's success: sharing the strategic direction of the organisation.

You probably expect that the direction that your organisation is going in, and why and how it's going to get there to be shared with you because, like most people, you want to contribute to something worthwhile. The direction that your organisation is going in is probably described by the strategic goals, objectives and plans to achieve them, and these may be cascaded down from your Chief Executive Officer or Managing Director, depending on the type of organisation you work for, to you and your colleagues via directors and managers who are more senior than you.

As well as understanding your organisation's goals, you also need to know how the objectives that your immediate line manager requires you to achieve fit with those wider goals. By clearly understanding this connection, you can appreciate how you're adding value and contributing to the success of your organisation. (The earlier section 'Clarifying how you add value' shows you how you can work out how to add value to your organisation.)

Just as you expect your immediate line manager to help you clarify how your objectives connect with your organisation's goals, your staff probably also expect the same from you.

 Being a visionary leader, and sharing your vision of how your team is going to carry out its work in the future, complements sharing the objectives or results you expect them to reach, because it enables them to see a more attractive way of working in the future.

Valuing having a vision

Have you ever flipped through a magazine or perhaps surfed the Internet and come across a picture of a location that grabs your attention so strongly that you start to dream of being there? Well, your vision needs to have this effect on your team . . . and more! Your vision, and how you share it, needs to be so attractive to members of your team that they become committed to making your vision become reality.

Your vision of your team depends upon your position and role in your organisation. Your vision may be for your whole organisation if you're the Managing Director, your function or department if you're a director or head of department, or your section or team if you're at another level in your organisation's management structure.

Your vision needs to fulfil the following roles:

- ✔ Present a picture or image of how you want your team to be at some point in the future.

- ✔ Describe what you want to create because this vision is focused on a future that is better than that what currently exists.

- ✔ Describe how your team will be working together in achieving its purpose or how it adds value to your organisation and/or its customers.

- ✔ Reflect and reinforce high standards of excellence regarding the work of your team in serving its customers, and how people in your team work together and with customers.

- ✔ Give a sense of what's possible: share it with enthusiasm and passion to inspire and encourage people to believe that they *can* create it.

- ✔ Be unique, important and worthwhile: people are more enthusiastic and committed about creating something that they want to be part of and which is important to them.

The value of your vision of how you see your team doing its work in the future lies in the quality of the vision you create and how well you share it with the people who report to you.

Creating your own vision

You may create a vision of how you want your team to be by yourself and then share it with them, or you may involve part of or all your team, depending on how many people comprise it, in creating the vision. The approach I describe for producing a vision is based on you doing it yourself, but you may follow the same steps in involving your team.

To create your vision for your team, first you need to clarify your team's purpose, and the required goals necessary to make a worthwhile contribution to the organisation as a whole. (You can discover how to clarify the purpose of your job and how you add value in the earlier section 'Clarifying how you add value'.) The overall purpose of your job is probably the same as that of your team because you're the leader of your team and are responsible for its work.

Keeping the purpose of your team in the back of your mind, start to create a picture or vision of how you see your team working in achieving its purpose by reflecting upon and answering the following questions.

You may prefer to draw a picture or write a few words that represent your vision for your team in answering the following questions:

1. **Get a notebook and copy the following questions, leaving enough space to answer them.** Then add your own questions to this list to help you to think about anything that's significant to you in creating your vision:

   - What will people in my team be doing?

   - How will members of the team be working together?

   - How will the team be working with and serving its customers and/or colleagues in other departments?

   - How will people be treated?

   - What impression will the team be making on the different groups of people it works for and with?

   - What will these different groups be saying about my team?

   - How will members of the team be feeling about their work and about each other?

2. When you've answered all the questions, reflect upon your answers to draw out the key words or themes that are significant to you.

3. Combine the significant words or themes to produce a short statement or paragraph that captures your vision of your team.

4. When you're satisfied with the statement or drawing that captures your vision, share it enthusiastically with your team so that they want to be part of it and make it come true.

5. Talk to your team regularly about the vision to reinforce what you're striving to create, and discuss the progress your team is making in creating it with them to acknowledge the team's achievements.

STORY

Fluffy white robes and slippers

I heard a Chief Executive of a hospice invite guests attending a fundraising ball to talk to her about contributing to the work of the hospice. I took up the invitation and subsequently met the Chief Executive to talk about the future plans for the hospice.

The Chief Executive described her vision for the hospice and I share with you now the picture that she described to me.

'My aim is to build a new hospice that fully utilises our position overlooking the valley and countryside for the benefit of our residents and staff. We will have six residential rooms, each with one wall of glass so that patients will be able to enjoy the panoramic view from their bed. Each room will also have its own secluded terrace so that residents and their families will be able to sit outside on fine days and enjoy the location and each others' company in private.

We will have a large treatment centre and a spa where people can enjoy a wide range of complimentary treatments provided by our wonderful staff. Residents and patients visiting for day care will mix with paying guests who are hiring the facilities (to generate income to sustain the hospice) in the spa and other areas. People will be shuffling around in white robes and slippers, enjoying and benefitting from the excellent skills of our staff and the facilities, and you won't be able to tell who are paying guests and who are residents or patients here for day care.'

This vision of caring for people, especially of building a community of people mingling together regardless of their health or wealth, inspired me to become a volunteer with the hospice and commit to sharing and using my expertise in how to build successful organisations.

The more you involve people in creating a vision, the more they feel part of it, own it and be committed to achieving it. A good starting point for involving your team in shaping and creating its future is to work with your staff in clarifying the team's purpose by working through the exercises in the earlier section 'Clarifying how you add value'. Just a simple step is then needed to involve them in working through the above exercise to create their vision for the team with you.

Expanding Your Sphere of Influence

I'm sure that, like most managers, you want to have more influence and control over your working life. For example, greater influence may mean:

- All the necessary resources to do everything you have to do being available without you needing to work extra hours.

- Everyone that you rely upon to provide the necessary information and so on to complete your work giving it to you on time, every time.

- Senior managers taking more notice of your views and opinions when making important decisions that affect you and your team.

In this section I encourage you to question and challenge yourself about the amount of influence you have, and work on expanding your sphere of influence over your work and, perhaps, in your organisation.

Discovering that you have more influence than you think

Your success in influencing people and situations is as much down to your mindset as to you having a particular skill! I use the term *mindset* in this context to mean a way of looking at or viewing something: in this case, the potential to influence a person or situation.

I describe two approaches that you can adopt – depending on which one of two different mindsets you may have – towards changes happening in your organisation that affect you. These two opposing approaches (one negative, one positive) demonstrate the importance of your mindset when you're trying to influence people:

✔ **I'm a victim of change.** If you see yourself as a victim of change, you don't think that you can do anything to influence whether or how changes are introduced. You typically wait for the change to happen and then cope as best you can with the consequences of the change.

✔ **I'm an agent of change.** If you see yourself as an agent of change, you're likely to look for opportunities to improve the performance of your organisation and to influence people to change processes, ways of working and so on, outside and within your area of responsibility.

Managing Directors and Chief Executives prefer people who work for them to be agents rather than victims of change.

Cultivate a positive mindset and attitude towards influencing people and being an agent of change by:

✔ Developing your ability to step outside of your comfort zone. Find out how to do so in Chapter 2.

✔ Recognising the words or phrases that typically come into your mind when you're faced with a problem, and then working on thinking about and using positive words and phrases whenever you encounter a difficult situation or notice an opportunity to bring a change about at work. You discover words and phrases that you can use to develop a positive attitude when facing and learning from adversity in Chapter 2.

Questioning your control

Like all employees, you have some but not total control over the work you do. Expanding your sphere of influence requires you to identify the factors that impact on your ability to work towards achieving the required results, and then invest your time and effort in having a greater influence over those factors. The following exercise helps you to do so:

1. **Draw three large concentric circles on a page in a notebook, as shown in Figure 4-4.**

2. **Take time to reflect on and list the factors that help you to be highly productive in doing your job.** Your list may include, for example, competent staff, reliable equipment and so on. Question yourself about whether you're making full use of these factors. For example, can you delegate more tasks to competent staff to increase your and their productivity.

3. **Now reflect on and identify the factors that hinder you from being highly productive in doing your job.** As you identify each factor, use the following guidelines to decide on the extent to which each factor is inside or outside of your control, and write each factor inside the relevant circle in your notebook:

   - **Within my control.** These factors are those about which you can decide what to do, when and how, without having to refer to or ask for permission from your manager or any other person.

   - **Within my sphere of influence.** These factors are those that aren't directly within your control, but you can influence somebody to act on them if you spend time gathering and analysing information, and make a robust argument for justifying that your proposals should be acted upon.

     You can influence most factors providing that you present a compelling and well-reasoned justification for action. For example, you may want to influence your attendance at (or the timing or duration of) meetings, or the level of priority that other departments give to your team's work.

   - **Outside of my control.** These factors are those that you can't influence regardless of how much time or effort you invest in trying to influence someone about them. Don't waste your time on the few factors that you can't influence or change, for example changes in legislation that affect the work of your team.

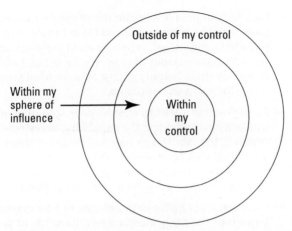

Figure 4-4: Factors within and outside your influence and control.

Targeting the people you want to influence

To be successful in expanding your sphere of influence, you need to be able to persuade people to change their minds, for example, about factors that are hindering your, or your team's, performance.

Identify the key decision-makers that you have to influence and try one of the following approaches to influence them to make the decision and/or take the action that you desire:

✔ Focus on building your relationship with individuals rather than focusing solely on what you want people to do for you.

✔ Work hard at really engaging people to create a mutual understanding about the actions that are necessary, important and worthwhile. Explain the benefits and consequences of taking/not taking action to the organisation as well as to you.

✔ Seek to gain people's commitment rather than just compliance to the action you want them to take. Try to find out what's important to people and how you can help them to achieve what they need – their motivations – as well as them helping you to achieve what you want. Strive for a win-win outcome.

✔ Build your networks to expand your sphere of influence by identifying who has the capability, knowledge and/or contacts to make things happen. (Some of these people aren't going to be in senior management positions.) Spend time with them, finding out what's important to them and showing a genuine interest in them.

✔ Question and challenge people about how urgent and important their requests and requirements of you and your team are to the success of the organisation. Be a critical friend by always striving to be positive in how you question and challenge people.

Be careful about using your power – whether this power is based on, for example, your authority, technical knowledge or expertise about how your organisation functions – to force people to do what you want them to do. You may win this battle but lose the next one: strive to avoid win-lose outcomes!

Chapter 5

Employing the Power of Engaging Leadership

*E*mployee engagement has received a lot of press over the last few years as a way of improving the performance of businesses and other organisations. In this chapter I define *employee engagement* and explain why engaging employees is so important to business and organisational performance. As leader of your team, you have the biggest impact on the extent to which your team members are engaged in contributing to the success of the overall organisation.

You find out about the four foundations for effectively engaging people – foundations that also underpin you being an engaging leader – and discover the secrets that enable engaging leaders to be brilliant at engaging everyone who works with them.

Engaging People: The Key to Unlocking Commitment

Businesses and other organisations are always on the lookout for ways of improving their performance, and employee engagement is increasingly seen as one such method. Many descriptions of employee engagement exist, but almost all recognise that the overall aim of employee engagement is as follows:

To encourage employees to contribute all that they are capable of contributing to the success of their organisation: to put all the skills, knowledge, expertise, ability to think and effort that is at their disposal into their work and into working with their colleagues, or put another way to go the extra mile.

The people who report to you have control over whether they apply *all* their knowledge, skills and so on in doing their work. Almost all employees want to do their job well and are at least compliant: they put enough effort into their job to achieve a reasonable level of performance, one that's more than good enough to avoid them being disciplined for not doing what's required of them. Many employees do a lot more than this and perform their job to a higher standard, but still don't do their job to their full capabilities.

You may sometimes have to use the authority that comes with your job to get less-motivated individuals to comply with your requirements and do their job to the standard of performance you expect from them, but each and every individual chooses whether to put in the extra effort required for high performance: every individual chooses whether to give you their total commitment. If you want all your staff to perform to their full capabilities, you have to be skilled in engaging them in ways that unlock their commitment. You find out more about engaging people in the later section 'Building the Foundations for Engaging People'.

The key to unlocking the commitment of people to perform a task to a high standard is engaging them in ways that mean that they take ownership of the task and hold themselves accountable for successfully completing it: they do the task to a high standard of performance because they commit to doing it to that standard.

Avoiding the black hole of meaningless work

People's work is a crucial part of their identity, as well as often being an important source of meaning. To test this notion, answer the following simple question:

When you initially meet a person, what's the first question you tend to ask to find out more about that person?

The question that most people ask is, 'What do you do?'.

Obtaining the answer not only gives you information about the person, but also enables you to relate to the person because – if you're like most people – you tend to associate certain characteristics with certain job titles such as barrister, engineer or accountant. Each of these roles has a certain meaning for you: perhaps, for example, you associate high earner, clever, articulate and so on with a barrister.

As well as job titles having meaning, the work that you do in carrying out your job is also a source of meaning for you: your work can be meaningful or meaningless . . . or somewhere in between:

- ✔ **Meaningful work.** When you view your work (whether a task or activity) as being meaningful, you see it as being important and worthwhile, and you're committed to doing it well. You're likely to be totally engrossed in doing the work because you apply all yourself – your knowledge, skills, expertise, thinking and so on – to making sure that you do it well.

- ✔ **Meaningless work.** When your work seems to be meaningless, you probably can't see a good reason for doing it well, or even at all. You're more likely to cut corners, delay or even not bother doing it until someone reminds you to do it.

Make sure that you avoid your staff perceiving their work as meaningless.

Making work meaningful

Your starting point for making work meaningful for your staff is to help them understand what's expected of them:

- ✔ Share your team's purpose and direction with the members. (Check out Chapter 4 for all about communicating the objectives and results that your team needs to achieve.)

- ✔ Explain what and how every member contributes to the success of the team.

Engaging members of your team to build mutual understanding is a great way to make work meaningful:

- ✔ Mutual understanding means that you and members of your team have a common and shared understanding about an issue, objective, priority, task, problem and so on: no room is left for misunderstandings!

- ✔ Mutual understanding involves you and members of your team agreeing on the importance and worthwhile nature of a particular objective, task or activity. When people have a common understanding that a task is important, they also have a common commitment to completing the task.

- ✔ Mutual understanding is created by everyone being involved in contributing ideas, views and thoughts, and asking searching questions to seek clarity. You and members of your team are more likely to:

  - Come to better decisions by involving the relevant people in making a decision simply because people see things from different perspectives, and contribute different ideas, highlight different potential problems and so on.

  - Work better together by people sharing their views on how well the team is working, and build a sense of camaraderie and team identity. (You discover in the preceding section that work is an important source of identity and meaning in people's lives. You can also find out a lot more about how to build teamwork in Part IV: 'Leading Different Types of Teams').

- ✔ Mutual understanding means involving people by having a genuine interest in them and asking for their thoughts and ideas, and listening to what they say; this approach reinforces the connection between you and them, and strengthens the relevant relationships.

Talking to a member of your team to enhance mutual understanding about the importance of a task or activity isn't the same as management by consensus. As team leader, you're ultimately accountable for the decisions made and actions taken by your team, and at times you're going to need to make decisions that some team members disagree with. Involving people, however, enables them to:

> ✔ Better understand the reasons for your decision.
>
> ✔ Appreciate you seeking and considering their views.
>
> ✔ Give you a higher level of commitment than they would if you hadn't engaged them.

Realising that engaged people go the extra mile

Research into employee engagement has shown that employees expect their line manager to:

> ✔ Keep them well informed about what's happening in the organisation.
>
> ✔ Treat them well.
>
> ✔ Seek and listen to their ideas and opinions.
>
> ✔ Show an interest in their well-being.

Engaging your team to establish common and shared understandings about important objectives, tasks and activities, demonstrates that you respect and value your team members: you seek their views and take notice of what they say.

Engaging people involves much more than seeking their views: you need to engage them in conversations and establish what's worthwhile, which requires you to seek and consider what's important to each individual as well as to the organisation. Being an engaging leader requires you to have and show a genuine interest in the work-related needs, hopes, aspirations and concerns of each individual who reports to you as well as you being interested in your organisation's required objectives and results. In my experience, people reciprocate the genuine interest that I show in them, and you're likely to find that your team members are then more committed and go the extra mile towards achieving what you need them to.

Your focus in engaging work colleagues needs to be on working together to create optimum outcomes for everyone involved so that everyone is unified in striving to achieve common goals. Engaging people requires you to find out what's important to people and find ways of enabling them to fulfil their needs through working towards achieving the required objectives and results.

Building the Foundations for Engaging People

My description of engaging leadership is:

> *Engaging leaders engage their staff to enhance mutual understanding and commitment to work better together towards achieving their objectives.*

Engaging your staff so that they're always highly committed to working with you to achieve the necessary and expected goals is difficult for the following reasons:

- ✔ **People are different.** You can't treat everyone the same way to get the best from them, but you can act with integrity and in accord with your values. (Refer to Chapter 3 to discover how to clarify the values that are important to you and use them in working with people.)

- ✔ **People can change.** Their needs and motivations may change depending upon changes in their personal circumstances, such as an employee becoming a parent for the first time and wanting to spend more time at home.

- ✔ **People may react differently to changes in their work situation.** Individuals and groups may react differently to, for example, changes in organisational structures, systems and processes.

- ✔ **People can misunderstand.** Misunderstandings can easily occur about aims, objectives, decisions and actions, especially when people don't articulate their thoughts clearly and concisely, don't listen carefully or make assumptions.

To gain and sustain the commitment of your staff, you have to be highly skilled in engaging people so as to notice or discover the factors that are impacting upon them, or that have to be addressed. In the next four sections, you find out about the four foundations for effectively engaging people (these foundations also underpin you being an engaging leader):

- ✔ **Relating.** Really connect with individuals and groups by showing a genuine interest in them.

- ✔ **Proacting.** Share and seek information, and critique each others' thoughts by 'speaking your mind' and asking searching questions.

- ✔ **Sensing.** Switch on your senses to gather data and information about others' thoughts, emotions, needs and commitment to act.

- ✔ **Inter-interpreting.** Interpret and reinterpret data and information, including views and opinions, to create mutual understandings and commitment to act on work issues and problems.

These four foundations are intimately connected with each other and are sub-processes of the overall process of engaging people.

For you to be an engaging leader – someone who's effective at engaging staff and work colleagues – you have to become skilled in using these four sub-processes simultaneously.

Relating to people

Many people see their relationships as being stable and longlasting, but in fact the relationships between you and many of your work colleagues can change. You may have strong relationships with, perhaps, just a few individuals: you may not see or even speak to these people for many years, but you can pick up the relationship immediately and have a conversation as if you'd spoken only a few days before.

You have less strong relationships with most people: these relationships are less stable, or even fragile, simply because of how you both relate to one another. As a result of your interpretations of your experiences of each other, these types of relationships can change more quickly than you realise.

Relating to people is a more appropriate way of thinking about how you and your staff connect with each other (instead of thinking of stable *relationships*), because the term more effectively conveys the potential for, and rate of, change in the relationship. Here's my description of *relating* (to a person):

> *Connecting with a person through having, and demonstrating, a positive interest in them and their needs (as a human being).*

The benefits of developing your skills in relating to your work colleagues include the following:

✔ You're more likely to be conscious of the effect you have on people and that they have on you when you recognise that how people relate to each other is a dynamic, fluid process.

✔ You develop a better understanding of people when you have a genuine interest in them and find out more about them. You're more likely to develop more meaningful and important relationships through this approach.

✔ People show more interest in, and have a greater commitment to, helping you to achieve what you want when you demonstrate that you have a positive, genuine interest in them.

✔ People are more likely to acknowledge and accept your explanations of the need for changes in organisational structure, systems or policies that have an adverse effect on them if they appreciate that you have a genuine interest in them as individuals.

Strive to develop your skills in relating to people to really connect with them, and through this approach build mutual respect for one another and stronger, more meaningful, lasting relationships.

When you're relating effectively to your work colleagues, you've adopted the approach of 'working with' rather than 'doing to' them. 'Working with' a person is based on you having and showing total respect for people and striving to really understand them.

Work through the following exercise to examine those occasions when someone's adopted the approach of 'doing to' you rather than 'working with' you:

1. **Get a notebook and divide the page into four columns as in Table 5-1.**

2. **Write brief notes that describe situations in which you felt that a work colleague was 'doing to' you in the first column.**

3. **In the second column note brief details that describe what your work colleague did or said that caused**

you to feel that the person was 'doing to' rather than 'working with' you.

4. Describe the effect of your work colleague's behaviour on you in the third column.

5. Describe how you then related to the person as a result of the effect that she had on you.

I give examples in the first row to help you get started.

Table 5-1 'Doing to' Versus 'Working with' People			
Brief Details of the Situation	*Brief Details of What my Colleague Did or Said*	*The Effect on Me*	*How I Then Related to the Person*
The situation was a team meeting when I was giving a progress report on my project.	My boss interrupted me and spoke for me, but she didn't express what I wanted to say correctly.	I had mixed emotions of embarrassment, being undermined and anger with my manager – although I hid my emotions.	I feel that my boss undermines me every time she does this even though I suspect she thinks she's actually supporting me.

You've probably noticed that certain work colleagues often adopt an approach of 'doing to' you and others because they're trying to be helpful. Unfortunately, such good intentions are in fact unhelpful because they can have unintended consequences such as:

- Undermining a person's self-confidence.

- Taking responsibility off a person by, for example, speaking for her.

- Imposing the doer's views on people, which can be particularly damaging when done in meetings.

- Giving an impression that the doer is self-centred by promoting her own views and even herself, especially when this act is done in large meetings.

- Causing people to disconnect from the doer and undermine relationships with her.

Beware of unintentionally adopting an approach of 'doing to' rather than 'working with' your work colleagues, because your behaviour can have unintended consequences for them and for you. (You can find more on how to 'work with' people in Chapter 6.)

Being Captain Courageous: Speaking your mind

You may be wondering why I use the term 'Captain Courageous' for this section? My reason is simply because you need to have courage to speak your mind: to express your thoughts openly and honestly. In my experience many managers, including senior managers, don't openly and honestly express their thoughts in meetings.

'Speaking your mind' is more than being open and honest in expressing your thoughts because it also involves encouraging others to speak their mind: to express their thoughts. As thoughts may include questions as well as views and opinions, 'speaking your mind' may also involve critiquing the thoughts of your work colleagues, as well as encouraging them to critique your thoughts.

I've coined a new word for this combination of activities – *proacting* – because the word captures being proactive in prompting and having meaningful conversations to share and clarify thinking in order to make something happen. The purpose of you and your colleagues proacting – seeking, sharing and critiquing each others' thoughts – is to:

✔ Generate and clarify information.

✔ Use this information to enhance mutual understanding about, for example, a work issue or problem that then:

- Enables better decisions to be made.

- Generates commitment to take action to implement those decisions.

I encourage you to be courageous because expressing your thoughts and encouraging your colleagues to critique your thoughts is risky: you and/or they may feel embarrassed or threatened because:

✔ Your views about a work issue or problem may be significantly different to those of your colleagues.

✔ Your colleagues may cause you to question your thoughts and views.

✔ Both of these scenarios may happen in a meeting when other people, perhaps more senior managers, are observing or are involved in the conversation.

You may need to develop your self-confidence to handle the perceived risks of speaking openly and honestly (this self-confidence is explored in Chapter 2), and of being vulnerable to having your work colleagues question, critique and challenge your thoughts (see the later section 'Building strength through vulnerability'). You can discover in Chapter 6 how to develop the ability to be courageous in having meaningful conversations with work colleagues.

Be a great role model for the people who work with you by demonstrating your willingness to express your thoughts, critique others' thoughts and encourage your work colleagues to do the same in working with you.

Switching on your senses

Have you ever been so consumed by your thoughts that you fail to notice something? For example, your partner may be talking to you and you don't notice what she's saying until she criticises you for not listening! Or you're watching a drama on television and realise that you've missed an important incident, because your thoughts drifted to a real incident that you experienced earlier that day.

You don't consciously switch off your senses so that you don't notice things happening around you, but you're just not as well tuned into those senses as you could be.

In my experience, one of the main causes of people being disengaged at work is that they perceive that their manager doesn't give them enough attention, listen to them or show enough interest in their well-being.

One of the biggest compliments that you can give people is to give them your total attention, because by doing so you're demonstrating that you respect and value them.

To give a work colleague your total attention, you have to be good at *sensing* what's going on around you:

✔ **Bring yourself 'into the moment'.** Focus your attention on the here and now, on the person(s) you're working with at that moment.

✔ **Switch on your senses.** Bring your senses into a heightened state of awareness so that you're highly alert and attentive to what's going on around you. In particular, turning up or tuning in your visual and auditory senses is crucial for you to notice small and subtle changes in the person or people you're working with, as well as in yourself. (You can discover the importance of recognising your thoughts, feelings and behaviour and how they impact on other people in Chapter 2). Switching on your senses enables you to better notice nuances in another person's and your own:

• Emotions, especially from noticing the expressions on a person's face.

• Behaviour or body language.

- Energy, particularly regarding whether a person is enthusiastic or not about the issue or topic being discussed.

- Use of, and emphasis on, words to clarify and understand fully the meanings that the person's attempting to convey to you.

The purpose of switching on your senses is to gather data and information that you can then interpret to enhance your own understanding of people including:

✔ Their priorities.

✔ Their perspective on, and views about, an issue.

✔ Their level of enthusiasm or commitment to taking an agreed action.

You find out how to switch on your senses or, put another way, improve your *sensing* ability, in Chapter 6.

Creating shared meanings

I was recently working in Brazil and I used an interpreter to explain and help me to understand the meanings of the views and opinions expressed during meetings with groups of employees in a company that I was working for. Your staff and work colleagues expect you to be your own interpreter: they expect you to explain clearly the meaning of information you're sharing with them, such as the reason for decisions or actions that you want them to take.

Employees expect their line manager to seek and listen to their views: they want to contribute to making decisions. Members of your team also have a responsibility to you and their colleagues to be their own interpreters and clearly explain the meaning of their views and opinions.

As you can discover in the earlier section 'Making work meaningful', engaging members of your team in order to enhance mutual understanding is a great way of making work meaningful. Enhancing mutual understanding requires you and members of your team to create shared meanings: common and shared understanding about, for example, the causes of problems, the reasons for decisions, agreed actions and so on.

Creating shared meanings requires you and your work colleagues to do more than just be your own interpreters, however, so that you can clearly convey and explain your views. Creating shared meanings involves an activity or process that I describe as *inter-interpreting*, which involves the following:

- **Interpreting together.** This part of the process means helping each other to come to better understandings instead of imposing one's thoughts, perspectives or interpretation on another person.

- **Striving to acquire understanding from each other's perspectives as well as your own perspectives.** This activity is more than just being empathetic and more than appreciating how another person is feeling about an issue: it involves opening up your mind to different and new perspectives.

- **Working together to help each other to understand each other's thoughts.** To better understand each other's interpretations and meanings of the information that you're sharing with each other, you and your colleagues have to be each others' interpreter as well as your own interpreter!

- **Seeing things in a new or different light.** This activity helps to gain insights that enable you and your team to create new meanings that lead to better understandings of complex problems and better decision making.

You can find tips on how to be better at *inter-interpreting* in Chapter 6.

Knowing the Secrets of Engaging Leaders

You probably know someone who's brilliant at engaging people, but you're not sure quite why that person is so good. Well, the earlier section 'Building the Foundations for Engaging People' can help because it provides a clear understanding of how to engage your work colleagues and staff effectively.

This section adds to those foundations and provides you with two secrets of engaging leaders.

Being open to everything

'Being open to everything' means being open to the opinions, views, ideas, proposals, arguments and so on of the people you work with. Being open to others' views doesn't mean that you have to accept them, because you're bound to have your own views. Instead, 'being open' means having an open, rather than a closed, mind: being willing to at least consider others' views and opinions.

You can develop an open mind as follows:

- ✔ Recognise that you're not your thoughts: they're simply expressions of what's going on in your mind. You may be attached to some of them, but you don't have to be!

- ✔ Value contrasting perspectives that your work colleagues may have towards a work issue.

- ✔ See work colleagues who are questioning or challenging your views or decisions as critical friends: almost all will be acting with good intentions because they want to improve an aspect of work.

- ✔ Give people space and time to express themselves.

Building strength through vulnerability

You may think that encouraging your work colleagues to express their views openly and honestly is risky, because they may put you on the spot and you may not be sure about how to respond. More specifically, you may feel more vulnerable encouraging a colleague to question, critique or even challenge your point of view because they may:

- ✔ Highlight that you haven't thoroughly thought through a decision.

- ✔ Undermine your view.

- ✔ Prove you wrong!

I suggest that you have the courage to invite colleagues to be open and honest in conversations with you – and each other – because:

- ✔ Your role as a leader is to get to the right decision regarding a work issue or problem: you don't have to come up with the answer yourself!

- ✔ Only through encouraging your colleagues to:

  - • Share their ideas, suggestions and viewpoints, can you tap into their knowledge and expertise in, for example, solving complex problems.

  - • Question, critique and challenge your thinking, and that of their colleagues, can your team members develop their ability to improve how they think; and improving the quality of thinking leads to improved mutual understanding of work issues, better decisions, greater commitment and improved results.

- ✔ By setting an example that you're willing to have your views challenged and even proved wrong you can encourage your colleagues to take risks in expressing their views and have their own views challenged.

- ✔ You develop self-confidence and are more able to have 'difficult conversations' by being put on the spot and coping with potentially or actually being embarrassed.

Thinking precedes action and having the right thoughts precedes taking the right action. Work with your colleagues to improve the quality of thinking, create shared meanings and common understandings about work issues and problems to enable you (and them) to act to solve problems and achieve the desired results for all concerned.

You can discover in Chapter 9 how to be more vulnerable by coping with situations that you find embarrassing and threatening.

Chapter 6

Becoming an Engaging Leader

• •

In This Chapter

▶ Connecting effectively with your colleagues

▶ Standing out by speaking up

▶ Focusing everyone on success

▶ Building commitment

• •

*T*he great news is that you already have some skills in engaging people, and you can build on these skills to become an engaging leader. In Chapter 5, I show you the four foundations for engaging your team members: *relating* to people; *proacting* to seek, share and critique each others' thoughts; *sensing* – switching on your senses to gather data and information; and *inter-interpreting* – interpreting and reinterpreting together.

In this chapter you find out how to enhance and effectively deploy your skills in these four foundations, and how to engage people effectively. I also show you how your improved performance as an engaging leader is linked to building your personal confidence, maintaining focus and clarity within your team, and increasing your team members' commitment.

Recognising Your Existing Skills

Chapter 5 describes how the four foundations for engaging your staff are intimately connected with each other. They are sub-processes of the overall process or activity of engaging people, and to be brilliant at engaging people you have to become skilled in using these four sub-processes simultaneously.

Before I explore using each of the four foundation sub-processes in more detail, take a few minutes to reflect on situations when you were in a conversation with an individual or group of people in which one or more of the following events occurred:

- ✔ You were all totally engrossed in the conversation.

- ✔ Individual and group understanding of the subject were significantly enhanced.

- ✔ One or more 'aha!' moments happened: for example, when new insights were gained into the subject being discussed.

- ✔ The people involved experienced a strong sense of togetherness or camaraderie.

- ✔ A common commitment to act resulted from the conversation.

Now try the following exercise.

1. **Get a notebook and divide the page into three columns as shown in Table 6-1.**

2. **Write a brief description of the situation in which the first conversation occurred.**

3. **In the second column, list the actions that you took – briefly describe what you did or said – to make a valuable and meaningful contribution to this conversation.**

4. **Describe the effect that your contribution had on you and/or the other people involved, or the outcome of the meeting.**

5. **Repeat steps 2 to 4 for other situations that you identified.**

I give an example in the first row to help you get started.

Table 6-1	Examples of Situations When I Used Skills in Engaging People	
Brief Description of the Situation	*Brief Description of What I Did or Said that was a Significant Contribution to the Conversation*	*The Effect that it Had on Me and/or Other People Involved, and the Outcome*
Weekly team meeting in which I thought that we were, as normal, meandering off the topics and wasting time.	I pointed out that we were going off-track and I questioned whether this way of holding meetings was the most effective use of our time.	Some people were initially defensive about why they had introduced new topics, but my questions prompted the team to re-evaluate how well we were holding meetings, and we agreed changes to improve the productivity of the meetings.

Take a look at the notes you make in the second column: these comments are examples of the skills that you already possess in engaging people, and ones on which you can build to become an engaging leader.

Enhancing Relating to People

As I reveal in Chapter 5, most working relationships are less stable, and sometimes more fragile, than you and other people may realise; the way that you relate to, or connect with, each other changes due to your interpretations of your experiences of working together. You find out how to enhance your skills in relating to and connecting with your work colleagues in the next four sections.

'Working with' and not 'doing to' people

In my experience, people want to make a positive difference or contribution to the organisation that employs them. I explain in Chapter 5 that, in trying to contribute, some people may be too helpful in working with their colleagues in the sense that they take responsibility off, or undermine, them. Examples of actions – and the reasons for taking them – when you may notice colleagues (or even caught yourself) taking responsibility off people include:

- Interrupting a colleague and finishing his sentences by expressing what you think your colleague was going to say.

- Taking a task off a colleague, especially a less experienced one, because you know how to do the task better. You may indeed complete the task quicker, but your intervention stops the less experienced person from discovering how to do it correctly and may undermine his self-confidence.

These are examples of unintentionally 'doing to' rather than 'working with' people, but you may perceive that some people deliberately impose their views or actions!

Work on improving your approach to working with your colleagues by:

✔ Having and showing total respect for every individual: respect the rights that you and each person have such as:

   • The right to express your views and opinions.

   • The right to express how you feel.

   • The right to be listened to and heard.

   • The right to change your mind.

✔ Striving to get to know and really understand them. (Refer to the next section 'Having a genuine interest in others' to find out more about how to do this successfully.)

✔ Being empathetic: put yourself 'in their shoes' and try to appreciate things from the other person's perspective.

Having a genuine interest in others

You may sometimes find that showing a genuine interest in others is difficult. For example, in a work context you may have demanding targets or results that you have to achieve, and think that you have to focus all your attention and effort on achieving those results. Focusing in on your targets has a similar effect to looking down a telescope: you can clearly see your targets but you can't see much else!

From my experience of working in numerous organisations, 'silo management' – which is when departments become inward looking and don't consider the needs of, or how they impact on, other departments – tends to happen when managers of departments focus on achieving their own department's targets. In doing so, managers tend to become blinkered to the needs of, or how their work affects, their peers in other departments. I describe this effect in the later sidebar 'Hitting your KPIs'.

An unintended side effect of focusing on your own targets is like putting blinkers on a horse to prevent it being distracted in a race: you stop noticing and showing an interest in what's going on around you!

Practise developing a genuine interest in your work colleagues by:

✔ **Challenging yourself: 'How well do I really know each person?'** Ask yourself how well you know each person who works with you, especially the people who report directly to you. Can you accurately describe their personal circumstances, interests and hobbies, hopes and aspirations, any concerns about their work and so on? What makes them tick? If you don't know, invest time in finding out by talking to them.

✔ **Asking members of your team about whether they think that you show enough interest in them.** If your organisation has an appraisal process, invite each person who reports to you to give you honest feedback about how well you lead, support and work with them. If your organisation doesn't have an appraisal system, take the initiative to have informal conversations with each person to obtain their views about you.

✔ **Checking your plans.** Take a look at your schedule, plan or 'to do' lists for the last month and estimate how much time or how many activities were focused on people: getting to know or understand them better, train, develop, guide and support them, and so on. What insights do your findings tell you about how much of a genuine interest you show in people?

Reflect on the benefits and consequences of how often you're showing a genuine interest in people, especially if your initial assessment indicates that you're thinking about people issues less than 20 per cent of the time – depending on the size of your team.

Building strong connections

When you build strong connections with your work colleagues, you also construct strong bonds and more stable relationships with them and throughout your team.

1. **Refer to Figure 6-1 and get a notebook to draw a figure to represent how closely connected you are with the people who report to you.**

Hitting your KPIs

The most senior manager of a large business asked me to work within the company to enhance the quality of leadership in order to deliver improvements in business performance. I interviewed all the senior managers, many middle managers and a representative sample of employees to acquire an understanding of the factors affecting leadership and how well the company was functioning as an organisation.

I discovered that a lot of emphasis had been placed on clarifying and using key performance indicators (KPIs) over recent months. The effect was that managers were very clear about the results they were expected to achieve, and were primarily focused on hitting their own KPIs. As a result, although improvements in performance had been seen, the improvements weren't as great as was expected.

I also discovered that the emphasis on using KPIs to focus managers' attention and efforts on achieving the results expected of them was having unintended consequences. The following comments made by managers capture some of these consequences:

✔ 'Managers aren't working together as well as they used to and departments are becoming 'silos.'

✔ 'Some KPIs conflict with each other.'

✔ 'There isn't any collective responsibility among senior managers for the success of the business.'

The emphasis on KPIs was having both positive and negative effects on (and between) managers.

2. Draw a small circle in the centre of the page and write your name inside it.

3. Draw a small circle representing each person who reports to you around your circle and put their name in it, the position of each circle being closer to or farther away from your circle based on how strongly you're connected with the person.

4. For each close connection that you have with a person ask yourself:

   • What are the reasons for this connection?

   • What have I done to create this connection?

- How do I treat this person?

- How much time do I spend with the person?

5. **Repeat step 4 for the connections that you have with other people who are less close.**

List the actions that you take that help you to build close connections with people, and plan actions that you're going to take to show a genuine interest in and build strong connections with all the people who report to you. Repeat this exercise for other key people who you work with.

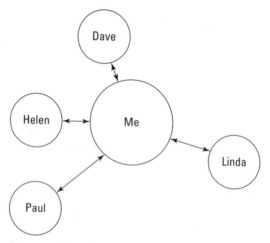

Figure 6-1: Illustration showing my connections with work colleagues.

You strengthen the connection between yourself and colleagues when they sense that you have a genuine interest in, and concern for, them. Plus, when you show this kind of interest, they're highly likely to reciprocate the interest in you, and the objectives and results that you're trying to achieve.

Being non-judgemental

You may not realise, but being judgemental – that is, forming an opinion about whether a person is good or bad – is all too easy, as is then allowing that opinion to affect adversely or unfairly how you treat the person.

I often use the following exercise on leadership development programmes to explore how easy becoming judgemental with people can be:

1. **Take a few moments to think about the person you most enjoy working with: a person who perhaps does great work, is helpful, reliable, takes initiative and so on.** Does the person's face appear in your mind?

2. **Now think about the person you least like to work with: someone who perhaps causes you a lot of problems, is difficult to work with, causes you to worry about work, who you like to avoid if you can and so on.** Can you see this person's face?

3. **Now reflect on how you work with each person, and question yourself about whether you're always fair regarding how you treat these two people.**

In my experience, virtually everyone who I ask to do this exercise agrees that they quickly see that they treat people differently. My concern is that you, if you also see different people, may unconsciously be carrying baggage about each person with you: views or opinions that prompt you automatically to treat people in a certain way.

For example, if you have an opinion that a person is difficult to work with, you may go into a conversation with the person about a problem with his work expecting to have a difficult conversation: you've already formed a judgement that the person is going to be difficult! If you do so, you're likely to contribute to causing a difficult situation because you don't have an open mind and may be less objective in asking questions about the problem and listening to what the person has to say.

Practise being non-judgemental by:

✔ Recognising and appreciating that each person is unique and, therefore, different. The best teams in my experience are those in which members have different perspectives, styles and ways of thinking because such diversity enables people to make a wide range of contributions to solving complex problems.

✔ Increasing your self-awareness by noticing the thoughts and opinions you have, or assumptions that you're making about individuals, and the implications of your opinions and assumptions for how you treat people. (Discover how to increase your self-awareness in the later section 'Being in the moment'.)

✔ Being empathetic towards each person; try to put yourself 'in the shoes' of a person to see things from, and to understand, their perspective. 'Doing so may involve you trying to understand their background, culture and so on. Improving your understanding of a work colleague's background may enable you to view his behaviour differently without lowering your standards regarding work or behaviour.

Developing the Courage to Speak Your Mind

I'm occasionally asked to work with groups that are very dysfunctional, and I've noticed that one of the main reasons for this condition is that people don't feel able to 'speak their minds' in order to resolve problems between members of the group. For such a situation, I put a lot of effort into finding an appropriate venue that would help to create the right environment for people to open up and share their thoughts with each other.

Although the physical environment is important, the crucial factor that determines whether people open up to each other by speaking their minds is the environment created by members of the group. You discover in the earlier section 'Enhancing Relating to People' that having and showing a genuine interest in a person helps you to understand that person: this approach is a good starting point in encouraging members of any group, especially a dysfunctional group, to work better together.

In this section I show you how to develop the courage to speak your mind as a complement to showing a genuine interest in people and enhancing your skills in engaging people in one-to-one and group situations.

Standing out from the crowd

You have probably noticed when walking in the countryside how sheep tend to follow each other: it appears that one decides to go in a certain direction and all the rest follow in a long line. I sometimes experience a similar condition in working with management groups: one person, often the most senior manager or strongest character in the group, proposes a decision and everyone goes along with it. This behaviour often leads to the condition known as *groupthink*.

Be aware of groupthink, where the thinking behind decisions goes unchallenged in a group, leading to poor-quality decision-making. Overcoming groupthink requires someone to have the courage to stand out from the crowd and speak his mind, to propose an alternative solution or challenge the proposed view.

Take the lead in speaking your mind in situations in which you experience groupthink, because by doing so you can:

✔ Assist the group to make more robust decisions by:

- Providing alternative and contrasting perspectives, options and solutions.

- Questioning the validity of proposals already put forward.

- Encouraging your colleagues to critique constructively, instead of automatically accepting your suggestions and proposals.

✔ Show leadership by being a role model and attempting to influence the rest of the group to follow your lead by sharing their views and critiquing the quality of thinking and decision-making.

✔ Challenge group norms of behaviour such as not questioning each other's views and encourage members of the group to strive continuously to improve how they work as a team.

Chapter 4 describes how the people who report to you expect you to be bold and lead with conviction. You're more likely to be bold and speak your mind when you're more sure of yourself, when you're confident that the thoughts you want to express are relevant and valid.

Being clear about the purpose of your job, the objectives and results that senior management expects you and your team to achieve, together with having a clear understanding of the goals and objectives of your department and/or organisation, enables you to be bolder and speak your mind. This clarity helps generate confidence that the points that you want to make and the questions you want to ask are relevant.

You probably perceive that 'standing out from the crowd' by expressing your thoughts – especially if they're different to the group's view or involve critiquing the views of a senior manager or strong character – would put you in a difficult situation. Refer to Chapter 2 to discover a technique to help you to be more comfortable with being uncomfortable and willing to address difficult situations.

Remaining aware of being dishonest

I don't think that you deliberately intend to be dishonest, but you may well have difficulty always being honest and saying what you really think! Complete the next exercise to check whether you do sometimes hold back.

Take a few minutes to reflect on situations in which you held back from expressing your honest views or opinions with an individual or group. The situation may be one that you experienced at work or in your personal life.

1. **Divide the page of a notebook into three columns as shown in Table 6-2.**

2. **Write a brief description of the situation in which you held back from expressing your true or honest thoughts.**

3. **Describe in the second column the thoughts that you had at the time.**

4. **Describe in the third column your reasons for not sharing your thoughts.**

5. **Repeat steps 2 to 4 for other similar situations that you identified.**

I provide a simple example in the first row to help you to get started.

Table 6-2 Examples of Situations When I Didn't Share My True or Honest Views

Brief Description of the Situation	Brief Description of What I Really Thought but Didn't Say	My Reason for Not Sharing My Thoughts or Opinions with the Individual/Group
One of the people who reports to me was again late for work by several minutes.	I thought the person shouldn't be late so often and should be better organised.	I didn't want to create a scene in which the person reacted badly and I wouldn't know how to cope with it.

People hold back from sharing what they really think for two main reasons: they want to avoid being embarrassed or threatened, or they don't want another person to feel embarrassed or threatened. I suspect that many people don't want to embarrass a person because they care for them.

You may feel threatened in a situation in which you say what you really think about a work colleague's performance, behaviour or attitude to work, and the person reacts angrily, verbally or emotionally towards you. Colleagues may feel threatened by you sharing your thoughts if they then have to do something that they don't want to do, your comments reflect badly on them or they feel that their job security is under threat.

Although certain occasions exist when saying what you really think isn't appropriate or worthwhile – such as when a work colleague makes a rare minor mistake on a task – you don't want to allow standards of work and behaviour to slip by holding back. You can find tips to help in the later section 'Coping with embarrassment and threat'.

Asking searching questions

Perhaps, like me, you've been discouraged from asking people searching questions, especially personal ones, because your parents or guardians think that doing so is impolite. You may have difficulty changing behaviour that you picked up when you were a child. The fact is, however, that as a team leader you're sometimes going to have to ask difficult questions.

In general, you're going to have one of three main aims when asking searching questions of work colleagues:

✔ To engage people with their own thoughts, by questioning the meaning of words, phrases and language that your colleagues are using in order to:

  • Enable them to think things through.

  • Clarify their thinking on the topic or subject being discussed.

  • Prompt them to question or test the assumptions that underpin their point of view.

✔ To gather more information to enable:

  • You to better understand people's points of view.

  • You and your team to improve your understanding of the topic, subject or problem being discussed.

✔ To encourage and promote the activity of asking searching questions as a valuable activity in decision-making.

Practise your ability to ask searching questions by:

✔ **Being curious.** Rekindle the hunger to understand and seek the truth that young children have, as demonstrated by them asking questions such as 'Why?'.

✔ **Keeping the conversation going.** A good question can be a statement such as 'Tell me about. . .' or 'Talk me through. . .'.

✔ **Using open questions.** People feel obliged to give you more information about the topic or subject you're discussing when you ask a question starting with *what, why, where, when, how, who* or *which*.

✔ **Becoming comfortable with silence.** Most people I've worked with don't like silence when they've asked a question, and ask another question or answer their own question within 20–30 seconds of asking the first question. Practise being silent for up to 90 seconds after you've asked a really good question.

✔ **Building up, not putting down.** Always have the positive intention of building up people instead of ridiculing, undermining, making them look foolish and so on in asking searching questions. People respect you when you act with integrity.

✔ **Remaining clear about your values or principles.** You're more likely to question and challenge others' views and even unacceptable behaviour in a group when you're clear about what's important to you. (Refer to Chapter 3 to find out how to clarify your values.)

✔ **Rising to your biggest challenge.** You may be the type of person who prefers to tackle the most difficult challenge straight away, or alternatively practise on less difficult situations or people first to progressively build your confidence. If you prefer the latter approach, start by asking searching questions of someone who's more receptive to being questioned or having his views challenged in order to develop your skills in framing questions.

✔ **Enhancing your ability to cope with potentially being embarrassed.** You may sometimes ask an inappropriate question such as one for which you should already know the answer. Checkout the later section 'Coping with embarrassment and threat' to find out how to handle being embarrassed.

Inviting challenge

One of the best ways of encouraging work colleagues to become used to others asking difficult questions and challenging their views is to set an example by inviting others to question and challenge your own views.

Be a good role model for inviting challenge by:

✔ Keeping an open mind to find the best solution to a problem. You may demonstrate this approach by admitting that you may not have the best suggestion or solution to the problem being considered, but that you want to get to the best solution.

✔ Maintaining a calm composure and vulnerability to having your views or decisions questioned or challenged. You discourage colleagues from sharing their views with you when you criticise them for taking the initiative to do so.

✔ Praising colleagues who effectively question and challenge your views and decisions.

Coping with embarrassment and threat

Chapter 5 describes how expressing your thoughts and encouraging your colleagues to critique your thoughts is risky, because you may feel embarrassed or threatened. You can also develop the courage to speak your mind by being able to cope with situations that you perceive to be embarrassing or threatening.

Here are a few ways to work on being able to cope with embarrassment and threat:

✔ **Recognise that embarrassment almost always fades with time.** Think about occasions when you felt embarrassed and you often realise that the emotion fades after an hour or two, or perhaps a day or two. Rarely are occasions so embarrassing that you're left with an emotional scar!

✔ **Nurture an 'I will survive' mentality.** You're more likely to put yourself into potentially embarrassing situations when you believe that you can cope with them. Use positive language such as 'I can. . .', 'I'm good' or 'I will survive' to talk up your self-esteem, or listen to a song that motivates or inspires you to help you to feel more positive.

- ✔ **Assess the risk**. If you're the sort of person who tends to worry when you do something wrong, such as asking an inappropriate question or making an inappropriate statement in a meeting, assess the real risk of doing so. For example, how many people do you know who were actually disciplined or dismissed for asking questions?

- ✔ **Recognise that every 'cloud has a silver lining'**. You learn by being exposed to difficult situations: you may not want deliberately to create situations in which you feel embarrassed, but you can certainly profit from them! (See Chapter 2 for ways to take lessons from adversity.)

Sensing for Success

Chapter 5 describes the importance of switching on your senses – especially your visual and auditory ones – so that you can notice subtle changes or nuances in another person's or your own:

- ✔ Emotions.

- ✔ Behaviour or body language.

- ✔ Energy or enthusiasm about the issue or topic being discussed.

- ✔ Emphasis on words that reflect that certain words have significant meaning.

You can then use the information gathered in this way to better understand your work colleagues, especially their commitment towards taking a certain course of action or doing a task that needs to be done to achieve an objective. In this section you discover techniques for using your senses more effectively.

Being in the moment

Take a few moments to relax. When you feel relaxed, turn your attention to your mind and notice how still your mind is and any thoughts that are on or come into your mind. . . .

You probably notice that your mind is still for only a few seconds before a thought jumps into it! Your active mind keeps grabbing your attention: you may sometimes find that this happens to such an extent that colleagues may occasionally notice that they don't have your attention, prompting them to enquire whether something's on your mind or even whether you're day dreaming! You yourself may sometimes notice that your attention is somewhere else – that is, not in the moment – when, for example, you're in a meeting and you miss comments made by your colleagues.

'Being in the moment' is the act of bringing your attention into the here and now, and enables you to focus your total attention on the person(s) you're working with at that moment.

Practise the following techniques to enhance your ability to bring yourself into the moment:

- **Calm your mind.** Let the thoughts that clutter your mind and disturb your attention slip away, and as new thoughts jump into your mind let each of them go. You may want to find a calm place to help you practise, but you can also practise this technique in public places such as on public transport.

- **Be aware of a single object.** Select a single object that you can see and increase your awareness of it but don't think about it. For example, I can see the shape of an apple on the computer I'm using: I'm increasing my awareness of the detail of the shape without associating lots of thoughts about apples with it. Practise holding your attention on a single object without thoughts entering your mind.

- **Relax your body.** Breathe slowly and relax your body. Let the excess energy that's causing your muscles – and you – to be tense slip away as you gently exhale each deep breath. You have probably heard the saying 'healthy body, healthy mind'; now you know another one 'calm body, calm mind'!

Seeing what others miss

'It's the little things that matter!' Such a comment is often made when describing exceptional quality of service provided by a restaurant, hotel and so on. I suggest the same is also true when you're effectively engaging a person: your work colleagues may rarely tell you how they feel and so noticing the subtle changes that other people miss, especially in a colleague's facial expressions, is crucial for you to become an engaging leader.

Try the following techniques to enhance your skills in seeing what others miss:

- ✔ **Keep your head up.** You can't notice subtle changes in a person's facial expressions if your radar isn't pointing in the right direction! Frequently looking at someone's eyes (without doing it so intensely that you make the person feel uncomfortable) enables you to connect with and relate to people.

  In my experience, people may avoid direct eye contact with you when they don't want to commit strongly to doing something.

  Watch for subtle changes in a person's facial expressions, especially around the eyes, for clues about what a person is really thinking. Use subtle changes that you notice in a person's behaviour, such as a raised eyebrow, as prompts to enquire about the person's views on, for example, a statement you've just made that may have prompted the reaction. Enquire what the reaction meant instead of making assumptions.

- ✔ **Work your peripheral view.** Practise noticing what's on the edge of your field of vision, especially when you're working with groups. You may detect subtle changes in people's body language and behaviour that you may otherwise miss.

- ✔ **Scan in and out.** Practise focusing your vision in and out so that you can zoom in on, for example, a person and notice what's on your peripheral vision almost simultaneously.

Listening for meaning: Getting behind language

You're most likely aware that you unconsciously ignore background noise at work, such as the soft drone of air conditioning fans. Your mind appears to tune out such noises so that you can get on with the work in hand. Although this skill is essential for good concentration, you need to develop your listening skills when talking directly with people.

Practise listening for details and meaning by tuning your hearing and attention in to the words and phrases that a work colleague's using during direct one-to-one conversations:

- ✔ 'Listen with your mind' by concentrating on trying to understand what the person means rather than primarily focusing on your own thoughts.

- ✔ Hold your attention at two levels; be 'in the moment' and attentive to the person while maintaining at the back of your mind an overview of what a successful outcome to the conversation is going to be.

- ✔ Notice subtle changes in the tone of the person's voice that indicates he's placing more emphasis on certain words and phrases: emphasis that suggests that these words and phrases have a significant meaning to the person.

- ✔ Look out for a colleague repeatedly using certain words and/or phrases in a conversation. Repeated use of the same phrase may indicate that your colleague thinks that you've not fully discussed or considered the issue. For example, if your colleague keeps on repeating the phrase 'there wasn't enough time' when discussing why a particular job wasn't completed on time with them, I suggest this probably means that he thinks that you've not considered this 'lack of time' issue to his satisfaction.

- ✔ Suspend judgement. If you interrupt someone, you've probably already decided that you know what your colleague's going to say or disagree with him.

- ✔ Listen for *how* people say things; and especially whether people are using jargon such as 'thinking outside the box', 'blue sky thinking,' and 'realising potential'. Make sure that you get people to explain what they mean in the particular situation and context.

- ✔ Listen for what people *don't* say; be alert to potentially different meanings of phrases and sentences that your colleague uses. For example, if a team member says the following sentence when explaining that he's experiencing problems obtaining information from another department: 'I tell them, but they don't take notice!' Does he mean:

- 'People in the other department deliberately ignore me.'
- 'I'm not very good at influencing people.'
- Or does he have another interpretation of the sentence?

Being Brilliant at Building Commitment

The key to unlocking the commitment of work colleagues so that they perform tasks to a high standard is engaging them. (Check out Chapter 5 for much more detail.) When engaged, people take ownership of tasks and hold themselves accountable for successfully completing their work.

Work colleagues taking ownership of tasks is the difference between them being committed to doing tasks to the best of their ability and them doing their work just 'okay' simply because they're being compliant with your requests/instructions. When colleagues are only being compliant, they probably don't do their work as well as they could, unless you have a great relationship with them and they want to really please you.

In this section, you discover how to build and maintain the commitment of work colleagues to do all their tasks to the best of their ability.

Starting from pole position

My use of a motor racing metaphor isn't meant to imply that you're in a race with your work colleagues to get what you want! As the leader of your team, however, you may feel as if you have to be (or even that others expect you to be) in pole position: as if you're in front of your team as regards setting the direction that you want your team to go in and expecting them to follow you. You may even think that you know best about what's required from your team and individual team members for them to contribute to achieving your team's objectives. While you do need to be clear about these objectives, this section shows some of the difficulties that adopting an approach of always being in pole position can create.

I've observed hundreds of managers holding conversations with a work colleague to agree actions to complete a task, or agree a change of behaviour, when a colleague is underperforming, in real work situations or as part of leadership development programmes. In my experience almost every manager adopts an approach that I describe as 'having the endpoint in mind', in which the managers:

✔ Focus on the action they want their colleague to take or the change that they want them to make in their behaviour.

✔ Attempt to influence the person to act or change behaviour by using what they, the manager, believes to be a logical argument or appropriate evidence of the need for their colleague to act or make the change.

This approach can backfire and fail to achieve your aims. When you adopt this approach, you're focusing on the endpoint or outcome that you want to achieve through having the conversation. Your attention is primarily on your own thoughts as you follow your plan of how you intend the conversation to proceed: you may miss or ignore important information that your colleague is sharing with you!

When you take this approach, a typical response to any comment that your colleague makes that indicates that he disagrees with your views is for you to reinforce your viewpoint by restating the need to act or change and/or by using (more) evidence that you consider appropriate. You focus on your own interpretation of, for example, your colleague's underperformance and on your own meaning or understanding of the reasons for this underperformance.

If you fail to provide sufficient reasons or evidence for taking action or making a change that your colleagues agree with, or if they interpret the evidence differently, you and they are going to have different interpretations and understanding regarding the need for them to act or change. If these different understandings persist, your colleagues probably end up with a lower commitment to act or change their behaviour than you want them to have.

Approaching conversations with colleagues by starting from pole position is more likely to result in people only being compliant with what you want them to do, instead of them being genuinely committed to act or change their behaviour. The next section presents a more effective approach.

Beginning from their grid position

Instead of 'starting from pole position' (see the preceding section), a more appropriate and successful place to start conversations with colleagues to gain their commitment to act or change their behaviour is to start from their *grid position*. This approach means beginning from where your colleagues are regarding their view about the need to act or change their behaviour rather than you focusing only on the outcome that you want to achieve.

You're more able to gain the commitment of colleagues to act or change their behaviour when you fully understand the reasons why they do or don't do something or behave as they do.

Here's how to start from your team member's grid position:

✔ Focus on and find out your colleague's views or position regarding the current situation, standard of performance, need to change and so on. Strive to find out whether, and how important and worthwhile, your colleague perceives the need to act or change his behaviour.

✔ Be alert and attentive to notice words and phrases that appear to have significant meaning to your colleague (check out the earlier section 'Listening for meaning: Getting behind language').

✔ Explore the meanings that your colleague attaches to these words so that you improve your understanding of his views or perspectives by using phrases such as:

- 'You mentioned [restate words] . . . what exactly do you mean?'

- 'You seem to put a lot of emphasis on [restate words].'

- 'It appears to me that [restate or paraphrase words] are significant to you.'

Focusing on winning together

Your aim in engaging work colleagues to 'go the extra mile' is to work together with a common commitment to achieve optimum outcomes for everyone involved (as I describe in Chapter 5). By doing so, everyone is unified in striving to achieve common objectives that directly or ultimately benefit your organisation, you and your staff.

Focusing on you working with one member of your team, striving to achieve a common objective, requires you and your colleague to arrive at a common and shared understanding about the importance of the objective and, depending on the difficulty of achieving it, the importance of tasks and activities that have to be done to achieve the objective. You *and* your colleague are *both* likely to be committed to achieving an objective, or doing a task or activity, when you agree that it is important and worthwhile because the objective or task is meaningful. (You found out about the dangers of work being meaningless to people in Chapter 5.)

Work with one of your colleagues to gain his commitment by agreeing that an objective, task or activity – or, perhaps, a change in his behaviour if he's underperforming – is important and worthwhile:

- ✔ Start from his grid position (see the preceding section for details).

- ✔ Explain the benefits of, for example, achieving an objective or doing a task, and the consequences of not doing it.

- ✔ Acquire a better understanding of each other's views and reasons for them.

- ✔ Gain new insights into the issue or problem, and identify more appropriate courses of action, through interpreting and reinterpreting together the views, ideas and information that you're sharing with each other.

- ✔ Notice any changes in your colleague's language during the conversation that indicates that he's accepted the need to act or change his behaviour, and that he's taking ownership and becoming committed to act or change.

Examples include a move away from negative phrases such as 'I can't. . .' and 'I won't . . .', towards more positive responses such as 'Would it be possible for me to. . .', 'How can I/we. . .' and 'Can I. . . ?'.

✔ Agree some actions to take to work together more successfully (read the next section for details).

Strive to engage your colleagues to enable them to achieve their aims and objectives by working with you to achieve the team's objectives.

Agreeing actions to drive success

Having a meaningful conversation with a colleague to gain his commitment to act or change behaviour is pointless if you don't also agree the action and a deadline for taking that action. Sometimes, depending on the situation, both your colleague and you need to take actions to demonstrate your commitment to achieving an objective and/or to working better together.

Try to be absolutely clear about actions to be taken by:

✔ Describing each action clearly and concisely.

✔ Naming who's going to take each action.

✔ Agreeing specific dates as deadlines for taking action; don't leave room for any misunderstandings.

✔ Agreeing a method and date for reviewing progress or measuring success.

Avoiding meaningless language

Avoid using vague or cryptic language in any conversations in which you're agreeing actions to be taken as a result of gaining a colleague's commitment to act. Such language can cause misunderstandings and, potentially, disagreements and/or ill feeling if your colleague doesn't act as you expected him to.

Be wary of the implications of allowing colleagues to use the language set out in Table 6-3 when they're describing actions they're going to take.

Table 6-3	Examples of Meaningless Language
Meaningless Language	**Implication**
Hopefully I...	I hope but I can't be certain!
I'll try...	Is trying good enough for you?
I'll do it by next month.	With at least 28 days in a month, which day is meant?
I intend to...	How committed does this comment sound to you?

Keeping on track

One of the best ways to sustain the commitment of colleagues to take the actions that have been agreed is to recognise the progress they're making and their achievements.

Keep work colleagues on track by:

✔ Holding reviews at the time and date that you agreed. Put the review dates into your diary to prompt you to take the lead in organising and holding reviews.

✔ Asking your colleague in review meetings to take the lead in describing the progress he's made, his achievements, difficulties experienced and how he's going to overcome them and so on.

✔ Using your colleague's name when praising him to build his self-esteem, so that he hears success and praise associated with his name.

✔ Constructively challenging your colleague if you think that he's not maintaining his commitment, and providing any additional support that he needs from you to succeed.

Chapter 7

Modifying Your Leadership Style

. . . .

In This Chapter

▶ Understanding why leading people is difficult

▶ Selecting an appropriate style for different situations

▶ Acting with integrity while modifying your style

. . . .

*A*s a manager you're going to encounter all sorts of different and varying situations and problems, and you need to be able to modify your preferred leadership style and approach as appropriate. In this chapter, you discover the main reasons why you may have difficulty leading people, and how different leadership styles affect the behaviour, attitudes and performance of your staff. In addition, I provide techniques for modifying your leadership style as you come up against different situations – so that your approach works for you and the people involved, while remaining authentic and acting with integrity.

Appreciating the Need for a Range of Styles

Many factors impact on the attitudes, behaviours and performance of the people who report to you and they may also have implications for your choice of leadership style. These factors include:

- ✔ **People themselves.** Every person is unique, each having a different personality, preferred ways of working, needs, hopes, concerns, range of competences and so on.

- ✔ **Nature of the work.** The work that your team does may be, for example, extremely varied or repetitive in nature, or involve members of your team working in close proximity to you or out of your sight for most of the time.

- ✔ **Culture of your organisation.** Culture is often described as 'the way things get done around here', but essentially culture is the prevailing values, beliefs, attitudes and behaviours of people within your organisation.

- ✔ **Your boss.** Your boss's leadership style and how it impacts on you and your team.

- ✔ **You.** How you feel (that is, your current emotional state), your attitude towards each person and how you've treated people in the past.

Although you may have a preferred or natural leadership style in working with your colleagues, you need to be conscious of that style and display flexibility in your approach:

- ✔ Be aware of the impact that your preferred style has on the attitudes, behaviours and performance of your work colleagues.

- ✔ Work on developing an engaging leadership style that enables you to modify your approach to working with colleagues, in order to gain their commitment to working with you to achieve objectives.

- ✔ When you do find that you need to change your style, make sure that you do so without compromising your integrity or the overall quality of your working relationships.

Wondering why you seem to get the problem people

You may have accepted a job and then subsequently found out that you've more than your fair share of people reporting to you who aren't behaving or performing to the standard you expect. Such a situation probably reflects that those people haven't been led or managed well in the past: the leadership style of your predecessor was inappropriate! You may well come across situations in which people think that they're performing their job well because they've never been told otherwise.

You may inherit people problems that were caused by your predecessor mis-managing people, through perhaps having standards that weren't good enough for the work your team does or giving inappropriate feedback (that is, leading people to believe that they're doing their jobs well when they're not!).

If you've been leading the people for several months and some of them aren't performing or behaving to the standards you expect of them, ask yourself the following question:

> *What am I doing or not doing that's contributing to the current problems regarding underperformance or unacceptable behaviour?*

Choosing horses for courses

Have you ever experienced a situation in which you treat two people the same way and find that they react differently to you? The same leadership style or approach may be effective in working with one person and less effective in working with another, which is just one reason why leading people can be difficult!

Consider modifying your leadership style when working with different people based on each individual's interests, needs, motives, preferred ways of working, skills and so on: all these attributes may affect the person's willingness and ability to do a required task. Leadership gurus Hersey and Blanchard describe this approach to leadership as *situational leadership* (in *Management of Organizational Behaviour, Utilizing Human Resources* (Prentice Hall)). They explain that leaders need to modify their directive and supportive styles of leadership to reflect the commitment and competence of each person who reports to them to do a particular task.

As well as the reasons I provide earlier in this section, other factors can also affect your choice of leadership style:

✔ How you're feeling at a given time and your attitude to work and each person who works for you.

✔ Your own boss's style. You may have a similar or different style of leadership compared to that of your boss, and any significant differences may cause tension or even conflict between you about how you need to be leading your staff. You may sometimes decide to modify your leadership approaches to reinforce each other, such as when you both want to propose enthusiastically a change in an organisational structure or process to senior managers.

When you experience tension or conflict with your boss due to significant differences in your styles, try to influence your boss to, for example, accept your approach to leading your team or even to modify her leadership style, and in doing so work better together. Check out Chapter 6 for how to enhance your skills in engaging people, including developing the courage to speak your mind, and Chapter 4 for more on increasing your sphere of influence.

Understanding Different Styles of Leadership

In this section, I look at two basic approaches to leadership – one challenging and focused on targets and the other supportive of individual people – and the need to be flexible as a manager. Modifying your leadership style helps you to engage your staff. Successfully engaging the people who report to you enables:

✔ You to gain their commitment to work together towards achieving the objectives that contribute to your organisation being successful.

✔ Them to fulfil their needs through working towards achieving those objectives.

To be brilliant at engaging people, you need to be skilled in the following:

- Relating to and connecting with people by having a genuine interest in them and their needs.

- Speaking your mind and asking searching questions.

- Noticing nuances in your own and other people's emotions, behaviour, enthusiasm and emphasis on words and language.

- Interpreting information together to create mutual understanding about, and commitment to, acting to achieve objectives, solve problems and so on.

Refer to Chapters 5 and 6 for more about these skills.

When you're skilled in engaging people, you can modify your leadership style without undermining your integrity because you're simultaneously focusing on achieving your team's objectives, being sensitive and responsive to the needs of each member of the team, and consistently acting authentically in accord with your values.

Exploring leadership styles

In my work on developing high performance cultures in organisations, I interview managers and groups of employees in order to identify the factors affecting organisational performance. Although all managers have their own individual style, the prevailing leadership style is one major factor that affects the attitudes, behaviours and performance of employees in many organisations.

The prevailing leadership styles can range from leaders being highly challenging to being highly supportive of employees. The behaviours of leaders who have a challenging approach to working with their colleagues include:

- Agreeing (or setting) objectives or targets that stretch people.

- Holding each person, clearly and consistently, accountable for achieving her objectives and results.

- Challenging unacceptable behaviour, language or performance promptly when it occurs.

The behaviours of leaders who have a supportive approach to working with their colleagues include:

- ✔ Spending time getting to know people individually and building a close working relationship with each of them.
- ✔ Praising people for doing a good job.
- ✔ Recognising and helping people to solve any problems they're experiencing in performing their job.

The above descriptions of leadership styles also reflect a different emphasis that leaders may place on achieving the objectives and results that they and their teams have to achieve compared to how much emphasis they place on people and their needs.

During a typical workday, you may find that you experience situations in which you need to modify your style or approach in order to place:

- ✔ Equal emphasis on achieving objectives and peoples' needs.
- ✔ More emphasis on achieving objectives.
- ✔ More emphasis on people as individuals and their needs during the situation.

Figure 7-1 provides examples of how you can modify your leadership approach to place different emphasis on achieving objectives and on the people who report to you in different situations.

Realising how styles impact on people and performance

Choosing the right leadership style for each situation can be difficult. For example, you need to get the balance correct between putting too much or too little emphasis on achieving objectives and/or the needs of individuals in a given situation, and challenging or supporting an individual too much or too little!

High

Style: Your focus in this situation is on achieving an important objective typically by an urgent deadline; you may be more directive by giving instructions, rather than consulting people about what to do, whilst still treating them with respect.	Style: You are focused on achieving objectives through involving people who report to, and work with, you to enable them to fulfil their needs through working towards achieving your team's objectives.
Style: Avoid being uninterested in achieving objectives and the needs of the people who work with you as your uninterest will achieve little and demotivate most people.	Style: Your focus in this situation is on the needs of individuals or your whole team with less attention, but not importance, given to progressing the achievement of work objectives. You may be building a person's self-confidence, developing their skills, discussing their concerns about a change in policy or procedure, and so on.

EMPHASIS ON ACHIEVING OBJECTIVES

Low   EMPHASIS ON PEOPLE   High

Adapted from Leadership Dilemmas – Grid Solutions *by Robert R. Blake and Anne Adams McCanse (Gulf).*

Figure 7-1: Examples of how you can modify your style in different situations.

TRY THIS

Here's an exercise that helps you to discover whether you get the right balance in this area.

1. **Get a notebook and divide the page into three columns as in Table 7-1.**

2. **Write a brief description of a situation in which you placed too much or too little emphasis on achieving an objective.**

3. **In the second column, briefly describe the action that you took or should have taken, or how you behaved.**

4. **Describe the effect of your action or inactivity or behaviour.**

5. **Repeat steps 2 to 4 for other situations that you identified.**

6. **Repeat steps 2 to 5 for situations in which you placed too much or too little emphasis on an individual who reports to you, and on that person's needs.**

7. **Reflect on the contents of the last two columns.**
Note how you want to improve your ability to work better with your colleagues to achieve objectives or to encourage and support them to achieve your standards, and meet their needs. (In Chapter 8, you can find out how to lead people towards achieving the standards of behaviour and performance that you expect.)

I provide an example in the first row to help you get started.

Table 7-1 Placing Too Much or Too Little Emphasis on Achieving Objectives and Individual Needs

Brief Description of the Situation	Action I Took or Didn't Take	The Effect of My Behaviour on the Team and/or Myself
I needed Jim to stay late to help complete an important job for a client. I asked Jim to stay back but he said he had other commitments.	I didn't explain the importance of the job and wasn't assertive enough in asking Jim to stay late.	I cut corners to hit the deadline and the job wasn't completed to the correct standard. I felt that I let the customer and myself down.

Unintended consequences!

Here are a couple of examples of leaders putting too much or too little emphasis on achieving results, and on the needs of the people who report to them.

Bill is the sort of guy who gets things done. He sets demanding targets for himself and his staff, and he's totally focused on achieving results. He has a tendency to overlook the feelings of people through being so focused on hitting his targets, and he can rub some people – especially those who have high expectations about how they should be treated – the wrong way. These people comply with Bill's demands, but don't give him their commitment. People who are target-driven and who aren't too concerned about how they're treated respond well to Bill's drive to achieve objectives and aren't adversely affected by his demanding and brusque manner.

Jane is a caring person who likes to get on well with all her colleagues. She gives people a lot of autonomy, and is grateful when anyone does a job for her and tends to thank people profusely even when jobs aren't demanding or difficult to complete. Although everyone thinks well of Jane's good intentions, some of her staff would like her to set more challenging targets and only praise staff when they do a job exceptionally well.

Many of Jane's staff also think that she doesn't challenge certain people enough, and that they take advantage of her caring approach. They think that standards are falling because certain Jane allows people to get away with doing work that's not good enough, and they resent having to work harder because she doesn't challenge those people.

Changing Your Leadership Style

In this section, you find out how to choose appropriate leadership styles that work for you and your colleagues.

Being true to yourself

Your work colleagues expect you to act with integrity! People generally have difficulty coping with a leader who acts inconsistently, for example, by displaying large, apparently irrational, swings in behaviour. For instance, if members of your team normally see you as being approachable, but you're occasionally brusque with them when you feel under pressure, they don't know how to respond to your changes in behaviour.

You confuse people if you act inconsistently by changing your behaviour without explanation, and if you change your mind about work priorities, standards of work and so on.

Make a conscious decision to modify your leadership style or approach based on the needs of each situation, but also ensure that you remain consistent by being authentic and by staying focused on the purpose of your job (Chapter 2 discusses the importance of authenticity as a leader). Clarity is vital in this aim, and Chapter 3 helps you get your values clear and Chapter 4 helps you clarify the purpose of your job.

Maintain your integrity by ensuring that how you act and behave with your work colleagues is always consistent with your values, while modifying your leadership style to reflect your work priorities and to meet the needs, motives, commitment, skills and so on of each individual.

Assessing first, choosing second

Your personal preferred or natural leadership style may cause you typically to adopt a certain approach to working with your colleagues, perhaps tending to be more supportive or more challenging. When deciding whether to modify your natural style or approach to dealing with different situations, consider the needs or requirements of each situation first before you decide how to modify your style.

The first step to assessing your approach to dealing with each situation is to assess yourself: for example, how your current work demands, emotional state and so on are affecting your approach to the situation and/or the people involved. Other needs or requirements that, perhaps, you can consider include:

✔ Work priorities such as the importance of tasks and the urgency to complete them.

✔ Needs of the people involved such as their personal needs, their desire to understand, their preferred approach to being led or managed and so on.

Focusing on outcomes

Focus on clarifying the outcomes that you want to achieve in assessing your approach to any given situation. The questions listed below may be relevant for you to ask yourself to clarify the outcomes that guide you in modifying your leadership style and adopting an appropriate approach to a given situation. You don't need to ask all or even most of the questions unless the situation is a significant event such as a major reorganisation of the work of your team:

- ✔ **'What work objective or result do I want to achieve?'** Am I absolutely clear in my own mind about what I want to achieve, and can I articulate this objective clearly?

- ✔ **'To what extent do I need to enthuse people?'** Should I be really enthusiastic and upbeat or adopt a quieter approach in explaining the importance of this work?

- ✔ **'What are the individual and/or collective needs of members of my team that I need them to fulfil with regard to the subject that I want to discuss with them?'** How clear am I about the interests, needs, preferences and so on of each person, and how am I going to address these?

- ✔ **'Do I need to sustain current levels of enthusiasm and commitment?'** How will the news that I need to share affect each person?

- ✔ **'To what extent do I need to raise the bar regarding standards of performance or behaviour?'** Do I need to be more challenging or supportive in working with each person to get the best out of them in this situation?

- ✔ **'What are the consequences of me adopting the wrong approach to this situation?'** Could I make the situation worse if I choose the wrong approach?

Excelling through trial and error

You need to work continually on enhancing your skills in modifying your leadership style to suit the needs of different situations by treating all situations as opportunities to expand your knowledge and experience. Use the following techniques to learn through trial and error:

✔ Step outside of your comfort zone and become more comfortable at being uncomfortable when challenging or supporting – depending on your natural style – your colleagues. (Refer to Chapter 2 to find more on being comfortable being uncomfortable.)

✔ Become more self-aware and sensitive in order to notice how you impact on your work colleagues through switching on your senses. (Check out Chapter 6 for all about the importance of using your senses.)

✔ Reflect on your experiences by using learning logs. (Chapter 2 has more on keeping a useful learning record.)

✔ Seek feedback from your colleagues about how your style affects them using the Johari Window (which I describe in Chapter 2).

Strive to develop a leadership style in which you're normally putting an equally high emphasis on the following:

✔ Achieving the objectives that you and your team have to achieve *and* enabling members of your team to satisfy their needs through working towards those objectives.

✔ Challenging *and* supporting everyone in your team to achieve and maintain high standards of work and behaviour in working together.

✔ Being bold in leading with conviction *and* being sensitive to appreciating how you're impacting on the attitudes and performance of each member of your team.

And make sure that you modify your style accordingly.

Chapter 8

Leading People to Peak Performance

*S*ometimes you're going to find that leading people is a joy: you admire how everyone pulls together to scale new heights of performance and teamwork. At other times, however, leading people can seem like an uphill battle as they falter and fail to deliver the performance you expect.

Throughout this chapter I employ the metaphor of climbing to help you discover how to encourage your staff to strive towards achieving peak performance by setting standards for them and acting promptly when individuals fail to achieve those standards. You find out how to tackle the thorny issues of unacceptable behaviour and performance, as well as how to use coaching to lead people to even better performance.

Being a Great Role Model

I'm sure that you look up to and admire certain leaders, those individuals who you aspire to be like and, maybe, have learnt from. Take a few minutes now to identify those leaders: perhaps you have direct experience of working with them or maybe you know of them only through books, magazines, television or other media.

Get a notebook and take a few minutes to capture your thoughts about each leader that you identify using the following statements as prompts:

- ✔ The name of the leader and the position held.
- ✔ The characteristics, attributes, principles, knowledge, skills or actions that you admire in this leader.
- ✔ The effect that this leader has had on you.

This simple exercise allows you to identify the impact that role models have had on you, and prompts you to see that you have a similar influence on your staff. You find out about the importance of setting and maintaining standards in the next two sections.

Flying your flag on the summit

You're responsible for setting and maintaining the standards of work, behaviour and performance of your whole team and every member of it: you're the standard-bearer for your team! You want your team to rally round your standards, uphold and protect them just as an army unites around and protects its distinctive flag in battle . . . even to the last man standing!

As the standard-bearer for your team, you also:

- ✔ Promote and uphold your own, your team's and your organisation's values.
- ✔ Represent, promote and uphold the purpose, objectives and requirements of your team within your organisation to enable people to achieve the objectives and results expected of them.
- ✔ Create a team identity that enables your team to feel part of something special. (You find out about the importance of team identity in Chapter 11.)

Be a bold standard-bearer and carry your flag high: 'fly it from the summit' so that what you and your team stand for, in terms of purpose, objectives, values and standards, can be seen by everyone in your team and all the people your team works with.

Do what I say not what I do!

Brian is a busy person, always dashing around from one meeting to another, jumping from one task to the next. His team is also busy and time is a precious commodity to all team members. Brian's team recognise that he is always struggling to keep to deadlines and that he doesn't like to be kept waiting. In fact, Brian makes a point of heavily criticising any member of his team who arrives late to any of his many team meetings. Unfortunately, Brian is often late for his own meetings!

Brian's late attendance at meetings has resulted in his staff paying lip service to his criticism of them: people continue to be late for meetings.

Being a leader can be extremely hard! You need to set the standards for others to follow: you have to be the person that you want others to become in terms of your team's values and standards regarding the quality of work, how members of your team work together and with colleagues in other departments and so on.

Setting the standard doesn't mean that you have to be able to do every task that every member of your team does. As people do their jobs every day, they become experts. The range of your responsibilities and the size of your team are likely to grow as you climb up your organisation's management structure and as your leadership and professional talents are recognised and appreciated, and you can't possibly be an expert in everything.

Your staff members are always watching you: your team and other work colleagues take more notice of – and tend to copy – your behaviour more than they take notice of what you say. Inspire members of your team to achieve your team's objectives by conveying your enthusiasm and commitment to succeed.

Avoiding the crevasse of double standards

You can't expect the people who report to you to work to or maintain standards that you don't keep yourself. Therefore, you need to avoid having double standards! Developing double standards without realising it is all too easy, just as Brian describes in the sidebar 'Do what I say not what I do!'.

Be careful of unintentionally allowing double standards:

- ✔ Don't make allowances for a person falling below your standard regarding an aspect of work or behaviour just because that person is highly skilled in other aspects. Some people are naturally more skilled or proficient at doing certain tasks than their colleagues, and you need to organise work to make best use of the collective talents of your team; but don't allow anyone to fall below the overall standards you expect everyone to achieve.

- ✔ Don't show favouritism towards certain team members. Be careful about turning a 'blind eye' towards people who fail to maintain the team's standards simply because you like them.

Noticing that the standards of work and behaviour in your team are falling can sometimes be difficult. Keep a constant lookout for early signs of standards falling because, just as a careless mountaineer can fall down a crevasse covered by snow, you need to discover problems sooner rather than later!

Acting Before Avalanches

When avalanches happen, they carry away everything in their path and bury it in deep snow. You may find that things come crashing down around you like an avalanche if you don't notice or ignore that standards are falling in your team as regards the work itself or how members of your team are behaving. Recovering from such problems can be difficult and time-consuming. I explore why and how you should avoid work avalanches in the next two sections.

Appreciating the dangers of delay

Putting off talking to someone about an unacceptable standard of work or behaviour can be all too easy, particularly if you:

✔ Are a busy person; you have good intentions regarding discussing the issue with the person but never get round to acting on them!

✔ Don't like having difficult conversations – and not many people do.

✔ Would be stepping outside of your comfort zone by raising the problem with the person.

Be aware of these common dangers of delaying taking action:

✔ **You accept a lower standard.** When people fail to meet your standard and you don't raise the problem promptly, they think that you're allowing it to happen. For example, if a person is occasionally late arriving at work and you don't raise the issue of timekeeping, that person may think that arriving late is okay. If you do not notice that the standard isn't being met, the affect on the other person is the same: he may assume you don't mind him arriving late.

✔ **You risk a bad apple infecting others.** If you allow one person's work or behaviour to fall below your expected standard, other team members may notice your inactivity and question why they should work to that standard when their colleague is being allowed to get away with not meeting it. For example, you may find that you've a growing timekeeping problem within your team if you don't take prompt action with a poor timekeeper.

✔ **Your credibility is damaged.** Members of your team who have high standards start to wonder why you don't take action: your credibility can be damaged by allowing a team member to fail to meet the team's standards.

✔ **Your job becomes more difficult.** Tackling the problem of unacceptable performance or behaviour becomes more difficult by not acting promptly because:

- The problem grows due to the 'bad apple' effect mentioned above.

- You may have to explain why you didn't act sooner; the person who's not meeting your standards may ask, 'Why didn't you raise this issue with me earlier?'.

Applying the golden rule of 'Now'

A golden rule to adopt regarding when to raise an unacceptable standard of work or behaviour is: *Do it Now!*

When you act as soon as you notice the problem, you can avoid the dangers mentioned in the preceding section and build your self-esteem by successfully tackling and dealing with problems with people – or people problems!

Another good general principle to adopt in leading people is to praise people in public and criticise them (constructively) in private. The following are the main benefits of adopting this principle:

✔ Praising people in public for achieving your standards means that:

- They get the public recognition they deserve.

- You reinforce high standards by talking publicly about a person achieving those standards.

- Their work colleagues recognise that they also have to achieve those standards if they want to be recognised for doing a good job.

✔ Constructively criticising people who aren't meeting your standards in private means that:

- You're treating them with respect.

- You don't unnecessarily embarrass them in public.

Raising issues of unacceptable standards of work or behaviour straightaway may mean the following, depending on the severity of the problem and the work context:

✔ Raising the issue the minute you notice the problem, such as in a one-to-one meeting or conversation with the person.

✔ Raising the issue at a time convenient to you the same day. For example, you may decide to delay raising the issue for a few hours if you have to complete an important task by an urgent deadline.

✔ Delaying raising the issue until the earliest time at which you can have a private conversation with the person.

✔ Delaying raising the issue until the earliest time that you can gather the relevant facts or evidence to determine the severity of the problem.

Two exceptions exist to raising unacceptable standards of behaviour only in private. You need to raise the problem as soon as you notice it happening in a meeting also involving other people when the behaviour is:

✔ So severe that you can't appear to ignore it for even a minute. An example is the use of abusive personal language.

✔ Typical of the behaviour of several members of the group, and you want to discuss the behaviour in the group because the group is malfunctioning as a result. In such situations, you may describe and discuss the behaviour without naming the last person to behave that way. A simple example is when people interrupt and talk over one another, which demonstrates that people aren't fully listening to what the others have to say.

Leading Under-performers Towards Your Peak

You find out in the earlier section 'Flying your flag on the summit' that, as the standard-bearer for your team, you're responsible for setting and maintaining the standards of work, behaviour and performance of your whole team and everyone in it! Getting everyone in your team to own and work to your standards can be a challenge. The next four sections describe how to lead people whose performance and/or behaviour is unacceptable with regard to your standards.

Working on commitment and capability

Your approach to working with a person who fails to meet your standards for work or behaviour is affected by your assessment of the person's:

- ✔ Capability to achieve the standard.

- ✔ Commitment to do the task to the required standard or behave in accord with your values or standards.

The capability of people to do a particular task to the standard required depends on several factors including their knowledge, skills, experience, the ability to think through complex tasks or problems, and so on. The commitment of people to do a particular task depends on the importance that they attach to the task, whether they like or dislike doing it, how easy or difficult the task is for them to do, and so on.

In some situations, you may be tempted to be satisfied when an underperforming person simply complies with your requirements, but I encourage you always to strive to gain a person's commitment to meeting the required standards because:

- ✔ Committed people are more likely to achieve the standard.

- ✔ Committed people allow you to have confidence that they're going to achieve and maintain the standard.

- ✔ Committed people are easier to manage: you don't have to monitor that they're meeting the standard as much as you do if they're not committed.

Check out Chapter 5 for more on the importance of engaging people so that they take ownership of (and commit to) the task and hold themselves accountable for successfully completing it. Chapter 6 shows you how to hold conversations to become brilliant at building commitment.

Figure 8-1 summarises four different approaches to leading a person, whose performance or behaviour is unacceptable, towards peak performance based on your assessment of the person's capability and commitment to do a given task.

HIGH

	GUIDE and DEVELOP	FOCUS and encourage AUTONOMY
Commitment	ENGAGE and provide DIRECTION	ENTHUSE

LOW　　　　　　　　Capability　　　　　　HIGH

(This model is based on the original work pioneered by Hersey and Blanchard on situational leadership. For more information on how situational leadership has been applied to executive coaching by Hersey and Chevalier refer to Coaching for Leadership, 2nd Edition (Pfeiffer).)

Figure 8-1: Approaches to working with people based on their commitment and capabilities.

You can take four different approaches to leading a person. These are to:

✔ **Enthuse** (when someone is highly capable, but has low commitment to doing the task) the person by:

- Clarifying the reasons why the person isn't committed by exploring whether he has any expectations or needs regarding the job that aren't being met.

- Explaining the importance of the task and the reasons why you want the person to do it.

- Recognising the person's knowledge, skills and so on that are particularly relevant to completing the task.

- Helping the person to understand that doing the task to the required standard will enable him to make progress towards satisfying any unmet needs or expectations that he has about the job or role in the organisation.

- Agreeing actions and deadlines, and how progress is to be measured.

- Thanking the person for using his abilities.

✔ **Engage and provide direction** (when the commitment and capability of a person to do a task are both low) by:

- Exploring whether any expectations aren't being met.

- Clarifying how the person feels about how he's doing the job, showing an interest in his sense of self-esteem and the reasons for his view.

- Looking for ways for building the person's self esteem by agreeing small steps or actions that slightly stretch his ability but that he's likely to complete successfully – with your support if necessary – so that you can recognise and praise even slight progress.

- Agreeing actions or tasks that progressively stretch the person as his confidence increases.

- Providing on-going support to develop the person's ability and provide feedback emphasising his achievements (use the person's name when praising him).

✔ **Guide and develop** (when a person is highly committed, but has low capability to do the task) the person by:

- Explaining the main steps to complete the task.

- Encouraging the person to ask questions, and ask your own, to ensure that he clearly understands what you require.

- Agreeing milestones and deadlines when you want the person to report and discuss progress with you.

- Being available for reference.

- Praising achievements and using problems as opportunities for the person to grow and develop his capabilities.

✔ **Focus and encourage autonomy** (when the commitment and capability of a person to do a task are both high) by:

- Agreeing the objective or outcome and deadline to be achieved without discussing the method.

- Providing enough autonomy for the person to make his own decisions and take action to achieve the objective.

Be careful to avoid taking highly committed and capable people for granted: remember to thank people for showing a high level of commitment and doing their job well.

Approaching cliffhanger conversations

Most leaders dislike having conversations with people whose performance or behaviour is unacceptable. I call these conversations 'cliffhangers' because you:

✔ Are concerned that you may lose your grip on yourself and lose control of your emotions.

✔ Fear that you may slip up in what you intend to say, say the wrong thing and not achieve the intended outcome.

✔ Expect that the conversation may sometimes be on a knife edge: tense and uncomfortable.

✔ Perceive that the consequences of the conversation going wrong are huge – and it looks a long way down!

Here are guidelines to help you plan how to have really meaningful and successful conversations with someone who's not doing the job to your required standard.

✔ Preparing yourself:

- Be crystal clear about the standards you expect your work colleagues to achieve.

- Be objective but non-judgemental. (Chapter 6 shows that being judgemental can cause you to make the conversation difficult by, for example, expecting the person to be difficult.)

- Switch on your senses to enable you to give the person your total attention. (You discover the benefits and how to switch on your senses in Chapters 5 and 6.)

✔ Preparing your kit:

- Collect all relevant facts and evidence while keeping an open mind that further relevant evidence may be shared with you during your conversation.

- Clarify any gap between the standard expected and the current level of performance or behaviour as indicated by the evidence, while being responsive to fresh evidence being shared with you in the conversation.

- Consider how the person prefers to be treated. For example, some people like to get straight to the point in conversations whereas others prefer to talk around and lead up to a key issue.

- Be clear about the outcomes you want to achieve from the conversation including any actions that will demonstrate the person is capable and committed to do the task.

✔ Be wary of third party opinions:

- Sometimes you may have to seek the views of colleagues in obtaining facts and evidence about a person's performance or behaviour such as when the person is a member of a project group that doesn't include you. Check whether the work colleagues are giving you subjective opinions or solid facts: opinions can be challenged much easier than facts.

- Ask your colleagues' permission to reveal, if necessary during your intended conversation, that they're the source of the information. If they don't give you their permission, be wary of using the evidence: you may decide that you have to use it, but the credibility of the information may be challenged and undermined if you can't justify it.

Roping people into improvements

Spend time and work with people who are failing to meet your standards so that they identify and understand the gap between their current level of performance or behaviour and your required standard. Encourage them to come up with the actions necessary to bridge this gap so that they take ownership of, and are committed to, improving. (Flip to Chapter 6 for how to ask searching questions, listen carefully and interpret information when agreeing the importance of a particular objective or task.)

Be smart by agreeing improvements that are 'SMART':

- ✔ **Specific.** The outcome or actions agreed need to be so clear and concise that they can only be interpreted one way.

- ✔ **Measurable.** You both clearly understand how progress will be measured such as through observation, measuring outputs, progress reviews and so on.

- ✔ **Achievable.** Agree any support that you'll provide including 'on or off-the-job' training, access to you for advice and so on.

- ✔ **Relevant.** All improvements should contribute to the individual, and/or your team and even the organisation being more successful: if not, why are you seeking an improvement?

- ✔ **Time-based.** Agree dates and times for holding progress reviews rather than propose to hold reviews in one, two or more weeks, which is too vague and open to misunderstandings about deadlines.

People tend to achieve tasks when you agree deadlines as compared to when you leave actions open-ended!

Mapping progress towards peak performance

When working with people who fail to meet your standards, you need to demonstrate your commitment to encouraging them to achieve the required level of performance. Continue to challenge and support them following your initial conversation to discuss their performance.

Always put the date and time for conducting a progress review(s) straight into your diary system; that is, during or immediately after your conversation. This habit reminds you to hold the reviews, and forces you to think about moving or removing it from your diary and consider the implications of doing so.

Consider the following points when making decisions about the type and frequency of progress reviews to map how well a person is making progress towards the required standard:

✔ Recognising and reinforcing people's progress helps to sustain their commitment.

✔ Allowing space for people to learn from making mistakes may be risky, but 'trial and error' is an effective method of discovering how to do a job better. You may consider that taking a few well-considered risks is worthwhile to enable people who are committed to making improvements to learn through making their own decisions and taking action.

✔ Deciding whether any milestones or deadlines while completing the task are critical to achieve, and how to ensure that these are met.

Coaching the Good Towards Greatness

When trying to enhance the performance or behaviour of their staff, many leaders make the mistake of telling people what to do: the message often goes in one ear and out of the other one! People have to take *ownership* of the need for the change and become committed to putting the effort in to sustain a change in their performance or behaviour.

Your challenge in coaching the people who report to you is to have meaningful conversations with them so that they take ownership of and become committed to making the change . . . and, ideally, to managing themselves in achieving and sustaining the improvement.

My description of the role of coach is to:

> *Engage people in their own thinking to enable them to gain new insights and meanings that enhance their confidence and lead to better decisions, actions, behaviour and performance.*

You discover useful tips on how to coach individuals and even your whole team to be even better at what they do in the next three sections.

Taking a time out to coach

In basketball, coaches can call a time out to discuss tactics; you can do the same and you don't even have to stop the game! You can coach individual members or the whole team as part of your normal daily activities. You may think that you don't have the time to coach people every day, but you do because each opportunity may only take a few minutes.

Be on the lookout for opportunities to coach individuals and your team everyday.

Here are a few examples of the many opportunities you have to coach members of your team towards greatness:

- Ask a team member who brings a problem to you to also bring options with a recommendation for how to solve the problem. Talk though the proposal and praise the person if you agree with the recommendation. If you disagree, ask relevant questions to guide the person towards your preferred action. (Dip into Chapter 6 to find more on asking searching questions.)

  When you've done this process a few times and are agreeing with the recommendations being put to you, help people to see that they're solving the problems, and only need to come to you if a problem is exceptional or the consequences of taking the wrong action are significant.

- When you notice that a task hasn't been done to the required standard, ask the relevant person to look at the task, and assess and comment on whether it meets the required standard. Ask questions to help the person spot where or how the task is sub-standard, understand the consequences of it being wrong and describe the actions to take to do the task correctly this time and in future.

- Catch people doing a great job by walking around and talking to them about the work they're doing. Praising people in public boosts their self-esteem and reinforces the standards that you expect people to achieve.

- Hold a short review of the process at the end of a team meeting to agree strengths and actions to improve how well:

- People were prepared for the meeting.
- Time was used.
- Everyone was encouraged to contribute.
- People listened to each other.
- Decisions were made and clear actions agreed.
- The team hold each other accountable for taking agreed actions following a meeting.

Be a great coach by regularly helping people to think things through for themselves.

Choosing the right role

I adopt and fulfil several different roles as a coach when working with chief executives, directors and other senior managers, often during each meeting with them. My clients often don't notice that I'm changing my role because my movement from one to another is subtle in response to the issues they're raising or their emotions.

I describe a few coaching roles, and situations when you need to consider using them, in Table 8-1.

Table 8-1	Coaching Roles and When to Use Them
Advisor	You've more knowledge and expertise than the people who report to you in certain aspects of their work. Advising involves guiding a person towards the correct or right way of doing a task where a best way exists.
Partner	You work together in jointly solving a problem, sharing your expertise and ideas to enhance each other's understanding of the problem and arrive at a decision that you're both committed to taking.
Reflector	You listen carefully and reflect back your interpretations to the person to check and clarify the meanings they're trying to convey, perhaps acting as a sounding board for their proposals and/or offering different interpretations. Use this approach to help people refine their thinking on an issue and acquire new insights into, for example, how to build a more productive working relationship with a colleague.

Catalyst	You prompt and probe people's thinking by asking searching questions and listening intently to notice words and phrases that seem to have significant meaning to them and, through this approach, enhance their understanding of an issue or problem and the actions that they're going to take. Useful for helping colleagues to work through what is, for them, a particularly difficult or complex problem.
Critical friend	You challenge someone about his thinking and behaviour while having a genuine interest in him as an individual, providing moral support and acting with integrity. This approach is powerful for helping people to enhance their self-awareness, acquire insights into their motives, attitudes and behaviours, and how their behaviour is impacting on others, and to increase their self-accountability.

You need to be highly skilled as a coach or have a strong relationship with a person to be a critical friend. And remember always to have critical friends yourself – they're of huge value as you go through your career.

Practising what great coaches do

Be a great coach by:

- ✔ Having a genuine interest in helping people to grow and prosper.
- ✔ Giving people your total attention when you're with them.
- ✔ Encouraging people to fulfil their potential as all times.
- ✔ Keeping your mind open to all possibilities and avoiding being judgemental.
- ✔ Asking searching and difficult questions to enhance the quality of people's thinking, explore the reasons for their actions and so on.
- ✔ Listening intently to the language people are using and noticing words and phrases that have significant meanings for them.
- ✔ Sensing whether people are showing real commitment to do what is right or necessary.

✔ Speaking your mind; that is, having the courage to say what needs to be said rather than ducking issues or avoiding disagreements. Be willing to challenge people's motives and behaviour.

✔ Reinterpreting information shared between you and individuals to create new insights and meanings about problems, and the person's self-awareness and self-knowledge.

✔ Being vulnerable by remaining willing to have your views questioned and challenged, and acknowledging and saying when you're wrong.

✔ Having humility: you're not the focus of the conversation!

Be a great coach by developing and using great skills in engaging people. (You found out about the core processes for, and how to enhance your skills in, engaging people in Chapters 5 and 6.)

Part III
Leading People Through Change

'The trouble is that they _all_ want to be leaders.'

In this part . . .

You find out how to successfully lead and implement changes in your workplace in these chapters. From spotting opportunities for workplace change to finding out about the power of storytelling to reinforce a new culture, this part provides many tips on how to prevent and overcome typical problems experienced in introducing change into a workplace.

Chapter 9

Transforming Workplace Culture: A Leader's Approach

. . . .

In This Chapter

▶ Starting from the right place when making changes

▶ Producing your change plan

▶ Gaining commitment and dealing with resistance to your changes

. . . .

*A*s a successful leader or manager, you have to take the lead when introducing workplace changes, regardless of whether the decision to make the change is yours or you even agree with it.

In this chapter you explore why you often have to work on transforming your workplace culture when introducing changes, and I introduce a range of actions that help you. Also, you discover how to identify where to start in making a change and transforming culture, the dangers of 'initiative-itis', how to choose the right pace for change and how to handle problems that crop up along the way.

Knowing Where and How to Begin

Most changes start within organisations because someone, often a senior manager, perceives a problem that needs fixing or an opportunity to make improvements in performance or save money.

Instead of waiting to be told to make a change, always be on the lookout for opportunities to deliver improvements in your team's performance and productivity. Encourage your team to seek out similar improvements too, and ways in which it can work more efficiently with other teams and departments.

Spotting the opportunity for change

You can utilise several starting points for making workplace changes that improve an aspect of performance: for example, get members of your team around a table to discuss how well the team is performing. Depending on the type of work that your team does, possible starting points include the following:

- You recognise something unsatisfactory about your team members' attitudes, behaviours and/or the importance they place on, for example, a current standard, system, process or way of working for or with another work group or customers.

- You spot that a key performance indicator (KPI) that you use to measure the performance of your team isn't being achieved or can be improved. (Check out Chapter 4 for more on KPIs.)

- You see or hear that another team or department inside your organisation, or an external customer, is disappointed with the standard of service or products that your team is providing.

- You become aware of a proposed change in an information system or work process that's going to affect how your team works, and you want to ensure that your team's needs or requirements are fully considered in any such changes.

Don't assume that your staff and colleagues are automatically going to welcome and embrace your proposed workplace change. You're not going to achieve the expected improvements in performance or benefits if the people affected by the change don't fully embrace it and want to make it work.

Always think about the cultural implications regarding a proposed workplace change: consider doing a 'deep dive' to uncover the cultural effects of a making such a change by asking yourself, and better still the people involved, the following questions:

- ✔ What are people's attitudes towards the proposed change?
- ✔ How may they react or behave with regard to the proposed change?
- ✔ To what extent do they see the proposed change as being important or necessary?
- ✔ Will they believe in, and be committed to, what you're trying to do or achieve?
- ✔ Will they welcome or resist the proposed change?

Read the later sidebar 'I'm not getting buy-in!' to find out why one Managing Director decided to invest in transforming the culture of his company.

'I'm not getting buy-in!'

One of my clients had invested many thousands of pounds and numerous hours of managers' time in learning about and introducing new systems and processes to improve the performance of his business. This Managing Director realised, however, that the improvements he'd expected from adopting the changes weren't being achieved, because managers were unable to get each other and employees to 'buy-in' to the new systems. When people don't 'buy-in' to a workplace change, they typically don't take ownership of making the change a success, often keep working the same way that they're used to working, and may overtly or covertly criticise the new system.

He asked me to work with the senior management team to discover how to engage each other and employees

to build a high-performance culture. I consulted all the senior managers, as well as 10 per cent of the workforce to obtain their views about the senior management team and other issues that could be affecting the performance of the company. I then analysed all of the information I'd collected and shared the results of my analysis when working with the senior management team, individually and collectively, to build a high-performing team. I then supported senior managers to engage employees to transform the culture progressively throughout the company.

By transforming the company culture, the firm managed to bring about the expected improvements and build strong working relationships among the managers and between managers and employees.

Starting from where you are

When I have initial conversations with potential clients, I often hear senior managers say 'now is not the right time' to work on improving or building a high-performance culture – one in which everyone is striving to achieve high levels of performance. The most common reasons given include:

- ✔ **We have too much work.** Organisations in this situation have a healthy order or sales book, and managers think that they have to give all their attention to, and put all their efforts into, getting the work done instead of thinking about how to improve getting the work done.

- ✔ **We have too little work.** Managers think that they have to focus on winning more work and, perhaps, they don't have money to invest in building a high-performance culture.

- ✔ **We're experiencing low morale throughout the company.** Morale may be low due to the organisation underperforming, which has resulted in a ban on overtime, redundancies, a breakdown in negotiations over a wage rise and so on.

- ✔ **We already have poor relationships between employees and management.** Relationships may have broken down due to actions that managers or employees have taken in the past that led to mistrust between both groups. Actions may have included proposed or actual reorganisations, miscommunications, the prevailing style of management and so on.

Some managers may prefer to wait for things to be better before they invest time and effort in transforming culture, but the whole point of transforming culture is to make changes that generate improvements in productivity and performance . . . and often rebuild problematic relationships and improve staff morale!

The right time to start working on transforming culture is as soon as you notice evidence or symptoms that indicate that performance, attitudes or behaviour is below what you expect. This advice applies whether you're working within a small group, a large department or even a whole organisation.

Creating a Plan for Your Change

When you spot an opportunity for improvement and come up with an idea for a workplace change, you need to plan your approach carefully – for example, deciding on the start and end points – and take into account a number of potential problems.

Experiencing initiative fatigue!

Have you ever heard colleagues respond to finding out that management intends to introduce another change with comments such as, 'Here we go again!' or 'Oh no, not another initiative!'.

If so, your organisation is probably suffering from 'initiative-itis'.

'Initiative-itis' describes the symptom of an organisation having too many initiatives happening at the same time. As well as prompting scathing comments, 'initiative-itis' is also associated with one or more of the following characteristics:

- ✔ Limited resources, such as people's time, are spread too thinly across too many initiatives.

- ✔ Staff greet each new initiative with a degree of cynicism.

- ✔ Existing initiatives or projects aren't progressing as expected and several may be incomplete and have 'loose ends'.

- ✔ Employees see initiatives as something to be done in addition to the normal work of (managing) a team, department or organisation. Staff may even perceive that the activities associated with working on the proposed change are optional – something they have to do only when they have the time!

When faced with these attitudes, you have to think carefully about how you present and characterise the change. Be wary of being seen to treat the proposed change as just yet another initiative, or to allow others to perceive such work in that light. Staff mustn't see your proposed change as something that's optional, a low priority and only to be done after the normal work of the team or department has been completed.

Work on transforming the workplace culture on the basis of, 'This is how I am/we are going to lead and manage the team differently'. Bed new ways of working into how the team works rather than allowing different ways of working to be seen as optional 'bolt-ons'.

Celebrating people past and present

Focusing on the future and how you want things to be when making a workplace change is quite natural. After all, you're interested in the improvements or benefits you want to achieve and your attention is likely to be on how you want your staff to behave, for example:

- ✔ The new things you want them to do.
- ✔ The skills you need them to have.
- ✔ How you want them to act and behave differently.

Be careful, however, that you don't focus so much on the future that you forget to think about the past and present.

Recognise the contributions that people have made in the past, and the contributions that they continue to make to the performance of the team or department, because otherwise you may unintentionally cause people to feel unappreciated or undervalued.

Clarifying the start and end points

The extent of the change you introduce into the workplace – and the accompanying transformation in culture – can be small or huge. Your change may involve a small team altering a specific work procedure or a whole organisational change involving the transformation of the entire culture of the workforce. Whatever the size of the change, however, your approach to clarifying the start and end points is roughly the same: the main variable is the number of people affected by, and potentially involved in making, the change.

In the following two lists, I suggest questions you may want to ask to clarify the start and end points for your change. Clarify the start point by conducting an analysis of the current situation by asking questions such as the following:

✔ **What is the current level of performance regarding this process (or system)?** Examine quantitative (numeric) and collect qualitative (anecdotal) information about the effectiveness of the relevant process or system from people using or affected by it.

✔ **How is this process currently being carried out?** Involve members of your team in drawing a process map that describes each step in the process, and identify any bottlenecks, failures and so on in the process, and the reasons for them.

✔ **What are people's attitudes towards this process (or system)? How much importance do they place on complying with it?** People may not follow a process if they don't understand the reasons for and benefits of it, or indeed the consequences of not complying with it.

✔ **What is it about this process (or system) that makes life easy or difficult for people?** In my experience, most people tend to follow processes that are easy rather than difficult – and take shortcuts to make life easier for them!

✔ **What is it that people like or dislike about the process (or system)?**

Use the responses you receive to these and other relevant questions to gather information to help you thoroughly understand the practical and cultural issues regarding the situation or problem that you and your team are experiencing.

Here are a few questions you can ask to clarify the end point of your proposed change:

✔ **What about the current process (or system) is valued and needs to be maintained?**

✔ **What are the improvements in performance or outcomes that I want to achieve with regard to this process (or system)?** (You can discover how to be 'SMART' when clarifying improvements in Chapter 8.)

✔ What is the new process (or system) going to look like when working effectively? How is it to operate, and how is it going to change what people do or how they work?

✔ What, if anything, needs to be different regarding people's attitude towards, or the value or importance they place on, the process (or system)?

✔ What will be being achieved that's not currently being achieved by the process (or system)?

Use the answers to the above questions to produce a specification of the new process or system and a description of the attitudes, values and behaviours that you want to establish with regard to it.

Always ask the people affected for their views, hopes and concerns when you're addressing the points in these lists. That way, they can let you know their concerns, and you can get them involved in design and implementation; and you also always get more ownership and buy-in when you do it. Such dialogue will reinforce people's perceptions of your capabilities and interest in them.

Asking and answering the above and other relevant questions helps to involve your team in making the change happen because it:

✔ Enables you to access their knowledge, experience and expertise with regard to the process you're considering changing.

✔ Makes them feel valued (you sought their views and opinions).

✔ Helps them to take ownership of, and be more committed to, making the change happen effectively (they contributed to and shaped the new process).

Bridging the gap between old and new

When you've clarified the start and end points of your proposed change (as I describe in the preceding section), you find that you've established the gap that exists between:

> ✔ The current process or way of working and the proposed process.
>
> ✔ The existing and the required attitudes, behaviours and values of people with regard to that process.

To bridge these gaps, you need to produce and implement an action plan that addresses the practical and cultural aspects of your change. Make sure that this action plan describes each of the actions or steps that are to be taken to bridge the gap, the deadline for each action to be completed and the name of the person to be held accountable for ensuring that the action is taken. An example of such a plan is given in Table 9-1. The last column in the table is used to capture up-to-date information of the progress made in implementing the plan.

Consider questions such as those listed below when producing your plan:

✔ **What are the various options for bridging the gap?**

✔ **What actions need to be taken, and in what order, to bridge the gap?**

✔ **What criteria am I going to use to measure or evaluate whether the change has been successful (criteria may include numeric and anecdotal evidence)?**

✔ **Which options or actions best meet the success criteria?**

✔ **How acceptable are the proposed actions going to be to the people affected?**

✔ **What can go wrong regarding making the change, and how can I recognise early signs of failure?**

✔ **How am I going to ensure that the change is maintained?**

Table 9-1	A Plan for Change		
Action	*Deadline*	*Person Accountable*	*Progress*
Brief the project team on the specification requirements of the new process.	30th May	Me	

(continued)

Table 9-1 *(continued)*

Action	Deadline	Person Accountable	Progress
Produce the first draft of the process flow chart describing all steps in the process.	15th June	Project Leader	

Adopting Approaches for Minimising Resistance to Change

This section takes a look at some of the problems and objections that may follow your decision to implement a workplace change. However good your preparation and planning, you can still experience problems if you don't dive deep enough to uncover people's objections.

Choosing the right pace for change

When you've decided that a new process or system needs to be introduced, make sure that you think carefully about the best pace to use to implement that change in order to gain your staff's commitment to making and sustaining it.

'Start! Stop!'

A company manufactures bespoke high-quality products for use in extreme environments, and the design and manufacture of its products is highly complex. One of the challenges facing the company is how best to use design expertise: whether to invest engineers' time and effort into winning contracts, and designing and manufacturing products or into research and development (R&D) activities to improve the quality of service and products offered to clients.

This dilemma was a constant one for senior managers, with engineers being asked to switch their focus from manufacturing to R&D activities, and vice versa. R&D projects were started and then paused while engineers served the needs of manufacturing. Engineers were not only confused by these changes, but they also started to question the credibility of decision-making when repeatedly being told that R&D projects were important and then to stop working on them. Morale was being affected because people were unable to progress the work they were interested in and that was important to them.

On a leadership development programme, a senior manager realised that a better approach would be to maintain the commitment, and manage the work, of engineers by planning to progress R&D projects at a pace that also allowed the manufacturing needs to be served. The analogy of shifting the gears on a car was used to maintain and yet vary momentum, instead of parking projects and picking them up again.

You can make the correct decision about the need to make a change, only to find that your staff don't embrace it (or even reject it) because you're introducing the change too quickly for their liking. They need time to come to terms with how the change affects them. On the other hand, you can also take too much time to make a decision and introduce a change, thus causing members of your team to experience unnecessary, prolonged anxiety about the possible changes that may be coming their way.

Avoid being inconsistent by changing your mind regarding the changes you want to make: your inconsistency may confuse people. See the sidebar 'Start, Stop!' for an example.

Uncovering people's objections

People differ in how willing they are to discuss their concerns about a proposed change. Some people are keen to let you know about their objections, whereas others are likely to be more reluctant to speak up. You need to appreciate this reluctance if you want to uncover (and therefore address) all their worries. People's reticence can be due to the following fears:

- ✔ Sharing their objections with you in a group situation, because they feel embarrassed about colleagues knowing about their objection to a proposed change.

- ✔ Revealing an objection that's particularly important to them; you may find that that some people share their most important objection last with you.

Be prepared to keep asking '. . . and what else is concerning or worrying you about the proposed change?', to uncover all the objections that a person may have regarding a proposed change.

People may object to the way a change is introduced as well as to how the change may adversely affect them.

Getting buy-in from everyone

Few phrases are as relevant to the dilemma of introducing a workplace change as, 'You can't please all the people all the time!' Some people may find aspects of the proposed change attractive while others are concerned about those very same (or of course different) aspects.

You may find that gaining the buy-in and total commitment of everyone involved in a change is quite impossible, no matter how much time and effort you invest in explaining it and dealing with people's concerns.

Adopt slightly different approaches to getting buy-in from people, depending upon the extent to which individuals accept or resist the change:

✔ **The enthusiastic.** Harness the enthusiasm of people who want the change to happen, perhaps by making them responsible for a specific task.

✔ **The ambivalent.** Reinforce the benefits and explain the consequences of not making the proposed change to those who are neither enthusiastic nor pessimistic. Detail how progress is to be monitored and evaluated.

✔ **The resistant.** Listen carefully to, and address the concerns of, people who are resisting the proposed change. (Check out the later section 'Handling resistance to change' to find out how to work with these members of staff.)

Ask the people affected by a proposed change to describe or explain the issues that would help or hinder them when adopting the change. You can then use these factors to introduce the change in a way that helps people to adopt the change, while also addressing the hindrances.

Making change tentative

Successful leaders manage to mix a variety of characteristics. They need to be authentic as a leader (as I describe in Chapter 2) and act decisively, boldly and with conviction. They also need to gain the commitment of people to do a task by engaging them so that the task becomes meaningful, important and worthwhile to those involved.

You may think that being bold and decisive while simultaneously engaging people is a contradiction. Well, it isn't: you can say what you think, *and* listen attentively to people's views and opinions, *and* also work together to create new meanings and insights to solve problems and make changes in the workplace. If you handle a workplace change tactfully and tentatively, you can achieve all the following together:

✔ Be bold about sharing your purpose – what you're aiming to achieve; and your values – what's important to you.

✔ Engage people in helping to solve problems and shape changes.

✔ Be willing to make difficult decisions that are right for the organisation but may adversely affect some people.

To make the change tentative, implement your decision while remaining willing to modify your plan – including the actions and timing of it – in light of people's reactions. Consider modifying your plan if by doing so people embrace the change, make it happen and sustain the change more effectively.

When introducing a workplace change, avoid the following extremes:

- Being so forthright that people think or feel that you're imposing the change on them. Be aware of the implications of people making comments – especially behind your back – such as, 'It's pointless arguing with him because he (thinks he) is always right.'

- Being so tentative that you appear uncertain or unconvinced that the change is the right thing to do.

Handling resistance to change

People put a lot of effort into promoting and protecting the things that are important to them: that is why some people actively resist a change being introduced into the workplace if the change is going to affect them adversely or they feel they're being mistreated as to how the change is being introduced.

Don't be surprised if people 'dig their heels in' and push back if you attempt to force them to accept a workplace change that they're reluctant to accept.

Be positive, empathetic and support people who are reluctant or resistant towards your proposed change. Table 9-2 contains suggestions you can take to help people handle some of the factors causing them to resist, and to enable them to accept and embrace the change you intend to make.

Table 9-2	Typical Factors Causing People to Resist Changes and How You Can Work With Them
Factors Causing People to Resist Change	*Actions to Address These Factors and Encourage People to Accept the Change*
Fear of being exposed as inadequate or incompetent	Talk through any concerns and fears that people have regarding the proposed change.
	Build people's confidence by emphasising their achievements and competences, especially regarding other changes they've experienced.
	Provide training in the new system or procedure.
Fear of the unknown	Provide as much information as you can.
	Admit when you don't have all the answers, and commit to keeping people up-to-date as information becomes available.
Loss of status or control	Explore the reason for people holding such views, and acknowledge their concerns.
	Consider giving people extra responsibilities especially if you can use their talents in other ways.
	Be honest and frank with people if their position in the organisation is changing, including changes in reporting relationships – and clearly explain the reasons for the change.
More difficult personal circumstances such as travel arrangements, impact on home life and so on	Consider whether other arrangements can be made, at least temporarily, to offset personal difficulties and help the person make the transition to the new working arrangements.
Unreasonable attitudes and resistance or criticism of changes you want to make	Challenge people who are behaving unreasonably and explain the conse- quences of them continuing to behave unreasonably.

Listen attentively to people who want to share their objections to a proposed change. You may not want to hear these objections, because they present you with problems that you have to solve, but you need to know about them because they're going to affect how well people embrace, adopt and carry out your intended change.

Chapter 10

Reinforcing a New Culture: Maintaining Your Workplace Changes

*N*o doubt you've heard the saying, 'Old habits die hard.' Well, a frustrated manager may have coined this phrase, when experiencing problems with staff slipping back into old ways of working while she's trying to transform the culture of her work team. Getting people to change long-held practices is one thing, but you can also experience difficulties when working with staff to sustain the following:

✔ Changes you make to a system or process in the workplace.

✔ Positive attitudes towards, enthusiasm for and even the compliance of people with the change you've made, especially if the change isn't working as well as you expected.

In this chapter you find out how you personally have a major influence on your work colleagues' enthusiasm and commitment to maintaining a workplace change. I show you how to reinforce vital attitudes, behaviours and values — that is, the workplace culture — in order to ensure that your change continues to be a success. You also discover what you need to pay attention to, in order to provide the 'scaffolding' to help people sustain the changes you want them to make and keep everyone involved on the right track.

Walking the Talk: Leading by Example

By encouraging you to 'walk the talk', I'm not suggesting that you waste time wandering around generally chatting to staff, but that your behaviour backs up your words. When you've implemented a change, I'm asking you to do the following:

- ✔ Demonstrate your commitment to ensuring that the change is a success, by making sure that your actions and behaviour reinforce what you're saying about the change you've made.

- ✔ Be how you want others to be regarding the change, because 'being' is more than 'doing': 'being' includes how you behave and how you are — that is, your presence — and remaining aware of how you impact on people.

- ✔ Keep in touch with how the people involved in, and affected by, your change think, feel and are acting as regards the change.

Catch people doing things right! As well as looking out for evidence of problems, also make sure that you spot what people are doing right when adopting a change in the workplace.

You find out how to 'walk the talk' to reinforce and embed the attitudes, values and behaviours required to ensure that your change is a success in the next three sections.

Being a visible leader

Face-to-face contact is perhaps the most effective way of influencing someone (or a small group) to sustain a workplace change. In this way you can:

✔ Convey your enthusiasm and conviction to make the
change a success directly to the person.

✔ Notice the effect that you're having on the person.

✔ Assess the willingness of the person to sustain the
change.

✔ Listen to and address any on-going or new concerns or
objections that person has about the change.

Invest in spending your time with, and giving your attention
to, people directly involved in making a workplace change.

To be honest, you really don't have any option, because you
invest your time in ensuring the change is being adopted and
maintained or spend your time finding out why the change
hasn't worked, trying to correct mistakes and resolve problems
that the change caused.

Remain conscious of the danger of becoming 'out of sight, out
of mind': convey your commitment to making the change a
success by maintaining your visibility.

Using the power of story-telling

People love to relate anecdotes and tell stories in all walks of
life, and the workplace is no exception. In fact, story-telling is
a more natural and important part of people's daily lives than
you may appreciate:

✔ Parents tell their children nursery rhymes and bedtime
stories, some of which contain important meanings or
messages about life.

✔ Friends and family members recount their daily
experiences as stories in conversations.

✔ Friends and work colleagues tell each other jokes, many
of which have a storyline.

✔ One generation hands down stories to the next in order
to pass on wisdom and sustain a culture.

You can use the power of story-telling to help maintain staff support for your workplace changes.

Take a few minutes to carry out the following exercise and reflect on your own experiences of the impact that story-telling can have on an organisation's culture:

1. **Divide the page of a notebook into 3 columns, as shown in Table 10-1.**

2. **In the first column, write a brief synopsis of a story or anecdote that you heard a work colleague tell about an event or situation in an organisation in which you both worked.**

3. **In the second column, write a few words that describe the main meaning or message that the person was attempting to convey through telling the story.**

4. **In the third column, capture the effect that you think telling the story had on reinforcing or changing your own or your work colleagues' attitudes, values or behaviour towards who or what the story was about.** It may be the organisation, a group or department in the organisation, senior management and so on.

5. **Repeat steps 3 to 5 for other experiences of story-telling that were significant for you.** I provide one example in the first row to help you get started.

6. **Examine the content of the third column to see what insights you gain about the power or impact of story-telling as a means of reinforcing and/or changing culture within work groups.**

Table 10-1	Examples of How Story-telling Reinforces or Changes People's Attitudes, Values or Behaviour	
Brief Synopsis of the Story	*Main Meaning or Message being Conveyed*	*Effect that Telling the Story Had on People*
A manufacturing company was closing down part of the operation and moving to a new site, but new improved equipment and facilities would be provided at the new site.	Senior managers can't be trusted.	Don't trust any senior managers – even though the individuals who had made the promises had left the company.
New equipment was not provided: senior managers had made several promises, including providing new equipment, but failed to deliver any of them.		

You may be surprised by the power that some stories have had in reinforcing or changing culture in organisations where you've worked, especially stories that people who have many years of experience of being employed in the relevant organisation tell regularly. Such stories are often about significant events or people and have a particularly strong meaning for those employees and, in my experience, are often about one of the following aspects (although you can probably add to the list after completing the above exercise):

- ✔ How good life used to be in the organisation – as perceived by the story-teller(s).

- ✔ Exceptionally good or bad leaders – and how they treated employees.

- ✔ An event that resulted in a major improvement or breakdown in relationships between management and employees.

- ✔ An achievement or occasion with which the story-teller is proud to be associated, such as winning a major contract or providing exceptional service to a customer.

Use story-telling to do the following:

- ✔ Paint a picture of how things are going to be when your proposed workplace change is working brilliantly: describe how people will feel about their work as well as what they'll be doing and achieving. (Refer to Chapter 4 to find out about the value of visioning and being a visionary leader.)

- ✔ Reinforce the progress being made in making and sustaining a change in the workplace. Talk about:

    - • Examples of problems experienced and how people overcame them.

    - • Improvements in performance that people are achieving due to the change.

    - • Feedback from other departments or customers to whom your team is providing a service, especially anecdotes that customers have provided regarding any noticeable improvements in the attitude or behaviour of members of your team.

> ✔ Share and reinforce good and exceptional practice or performance by a member of your team in adopting the new process or system.
>
> ✔ Encourage members of your team to tell their own stories about difficulties and successes experienced in adopting the change in the workplace.

Spotting people straying from the path

You may find that people stray from the path — the new way of working — because they:

> ✔ Aren't clear about where the path is leading.
>
> ✔ Are unsure about exactly what they're expected to do.
>
> ✔ Don't have the skills or tools to keep up with the pace.
>
> ✔ Don't want to change, and/or don't want the new process or system to work.

Chapters 5 and 6 cover the importance of, and how to become skilled in, engaging people to gain their commitment to do a task. You can use these same approaches and skills to ensure that people embrace and sustain a change in the workplace. Engaging people effectively in making a change enables you to address the first three factors mentioned in the preceding list, but the last issue — spotting people who don't want to change — may be harder to detect, especially if people are unwilling to tell you what they really think about making the change work.

A person who actively undermines a workplace change, but presents the image of complying with or even embracing the change, may be particularly difficult (for you) to manage.

People can actively undermine a change by employing one or more of the following types of behaviour:

> ✔ Arguing to their colleagues that the change is unnecessary.
>
> ✔ Telling their colleagues that the change won't work and is 'doomed to fail'.

✔ Proposing that the change is the 'thin end of the wedge' and that work and conditions are going to become more difficult for them all.

✔ Emphasising problems experienced with the change to their colleagues.

Some of your staff may have extreme difficulty challenging a colleague who's actively undermining the change, especially if that person is a strong character.

Almost all people behave reasonably when treated fairly, but you need to be on the lookout for any evidence that a person may not be supporting, or is even undermining, your change. Look for any inconsistencies in what the person says (especially during one-to-one conversations and group meetings) and then actually does with regard to the change.

Use your skills in sensing commitment, particularly the highly developed skills of seeing 'what others may miss' and listening intensely, to notice when someone doesn't want to change. (Check out Chapter 6 for more on sensing commitment.)

Spotting people who are undermining your changes when not directly in your presence is the first step in tackling their behaviour. Chapter 8 shows you approaches that help you handle this problem, describes the golden rule of (acting) 'Now' and also details the dangers of delaying talking to a work colleague whose work or behaviour is unacceptable.

Paying Attention to the Right Things

Leading and managing people is difficult because so many things are competing for your attention, including:

✔ Ensuring that you achieve the objectives and results expected of you and your team.

✔ Organising people and work.

✔ Sticking to deadlines.

✔ Seeing to the needs and expectations of every member of your team.

✔ Solving problems and resolving disagreements or any relationship issues between members of your team.

✔ And so on, and so on. . . .

You also have to make sure that you pay enough attention to your introduced changes so that they're successful and maintained. The earlier section 'Walking the Talk: Leading by Example' describes how you personally have an impact on the enthusiasm and commitment of people to sustain a workplace change, whereas this section shows what you need to pay attention to in order to complement your personal impact.

Remembering that what gets measured gets done

Key performance indicators (KPIs) are vital in helping you to measure how effectively you're achieving your objectives. (Turn to Chapter 4 for more info on KPIs.) Well, you can also use these key performance measures to evaluate how well your workplace changes are working.

For example, if you're implementing a change in a production process to improve the quality of products coming off a production line, you may be interested in the following KPIs:

✔ Percentage of products produced within the product specification.

✔ Number of products that had to be reworked due to faulty workmanship in each team or step in the production process.

✔ Percentage, or value, of products scrapped.

✔ Number of faults, by type or cause (so that you can work on eradicating the source of the faults).

KPIs have three main uses:

✔ To inform an individual or group about the target or standard of performance that has to be achieved.

✔ To monitor progress in achieving the target or standard.

✔ To influence how people think and act regarding the specific target or standard of performance.

When implementing and sustaining a change in the workplace, you can use KPIs to reinforce important standards, attitudes and behaviour as follows:

- ✔ Display information about how well your team is achieving KPIs on visual display boards, using graphs to show trends in performance.

- ✔ Discuss KPIs with your team, highlighting achievements and focusing on aspects of performance that are below the required target or standard.

- ✔ Talk about good and bad examples of approaches/ attitudes towards preventing or solving problems and making the change a continued success.

Keeping everyone up-to-date

From the point of view of the staff potentially affected by or involved in planned workplace changes, 'no news is bad news'. In my experience, most people prefer (and indeed expect) to be kept informed about what's happening regarding changes in their work environment.

The problem is that people tend to fill a void in information if you don't provide enough up-to-date details about a proposed change. You may find people speculating about what you or senior managers intend to do and how this is going to affect them – and people often fear the worst! Don't be surprised to discover that the 'grapevine' – the informal process by which employees pass information, views and opinions to each other – is working against you and what you're trying to achieve by your intended changes.

Generally speaking, you can't inform people too much about a proposed workplace change . . . with one exception: the sharing of information or partially formed decisions that are likely to cause unnecessary concern or worry for employees.

Use regular briefing sessions with groups of up to 20 employees, depending on the number of employees affected by the change, in order to:

- ✔ Inform people about proposed changes.

- ✔ Explain and explore how effectively changes that have been introduced are working.

✔ Encourage people to ask questions and for you to answer them.

Use your line managers to reinforce key messages and answer questions with their own, probably smaller, groups of employees who report to them. Do inform employee representatives about changes, but use the management structure to convey and reinforce key messages to employees about a change.

To the people who report to them, line managers are the organisation and represent the organisation: line managers are, potentially, the greatest single influence on an employee who reports to them.

Reacting positively to crises

Sometimes you're going to find yourself in situations that aren't of your choosing but in which you need to choose your reaction. Trying to make the best of a bad job is far better than reacting negatively and complaining about the situation. When a workplace change that you've made goes badly wrong, you may feel that you're facing a crisis:

✔ Errors or faulty products have been made.

✔ The process stops, especially if it involves, for example, an information technology or production process.

✔ You're in the spotlight: the eyes of more senior managers and everyone around you are on you!

✔ You feel intense pressure on you to solve the problem.

Hearing about problems with a change you've made can be difficult. You may be the sort of person who remains calm in a crisis but, if not, try not to overreact or do or say something that you may later regret. Here are some suggestions:

✔ Use the diving motto – 'stop, think, breathe!' – to help you keep calm.

✔ Avoid blaming people – by all means hold people accountable, but recognise that people rarely deliberately make mistakes; recognising their good intentions helps you to deal with the problem without damaging your relationship with them.

✔ Critique a person's behaviour – what they did wrong or didn't do right – rather than criticising their personality. People can change their behaviour but not their personality.

✔ Focus on the future – on the actions to take, by when and by whom, to solve the problem.

✔ Help people to learn from their mistakes – ask searching questions to help people to think through what they could have done and, in the future, will do differently. (Refer to Chapter 6 to find out more about asking searching questions.)

Promoting good practice

Promoting good practice isn't about promoting someone who does a good job to a better position (although of course you're likely to promote people who consistently deliver high levels of performance and capability). Promoting good practice with regards to reinforcing a workplace change is about recognising and praising people who do the following:

✔ Demonstrate the most positive attitudes towards the changes being made.

✔ Place the same high level of importance as you do on the objectives, targets, standards of service and so on associated with the system, process or structure being changed.

✔ See problems experienced with the change as opportunities to make improvements and acquire knowledge and expertise about implementing changes into the workplace.

By recognising and praising good practice you can:

✔ Reinforce the attitudes, values and behaviours that you believe are important to:

• Ensure that the specific change that has been made is maintained.

• Sustain the success of your team.

✔ Let people know what's expected of them if they want to be recognised.

Part IV
Leading Teams

'If you want to be part of our leadership
team, you've got to be able to do this.'

In this part . . .

Do you want to know how to lead and build your team? Would you like to make your senior leadership team a great role model for the rest of your organisation? Step straight into this part. Discover many team building techniques and the characteristics that separate great teams from merely good teams.

Chapter 11

Leading Your Own Team

· ·

· ·

sk yourself the following question: can you succeed in your job without relying on other people? I suspect not, because the number of people whose work is so specialist and independent of the work going on around them is miniscule. Organisations are, by definition, collections, groups or teams of people who work together to achieve a purpose, often expressed as the organisation's goals, objectives or targets.

People don't work well as a team just because they happen to work together! Teamwork is exactly that: work. You need to work at building your team and lead team members to work at sustaining and improving teamwork, which is what this chapter is all about. You can use the team-building methods I describe in this chapter with any type of team, regardless of the context in which the team works. (For more detailed information on how to build and lead a senior management team check out Chapter 12.)

Creating a High-Performing Team

Clearly, high-performing teams are successful teams. But what is success? In situations where teams are in direct competition with each other – such as in football where the sole measure of success is winning matches – the high-performing teams are evident: they're at the top of their league. Knowing, however, whether your work team is high-performing is difficult, because you don't have other teams against which to compare performance directly. Your team may be successful in terms of achieving the expected objectives, but how do you know whether it's performing to its full potential? This section provides several approaches that you can take to identify and adopt the characteristics of high-performing teams.

One overall aspect of a successful team is usually apparent. A high-performing team has *synergy*: that is, its members work together in ways that enable them to:

✔ Achieve and sustain exceptionally high levels of performance or output.

✔ Improve productivity, and how they work together, continuously.

Dealing with 'we're okay: leave us alone'

In this section, I show you how to tackle an obstacle to high performance: complacency. Perhaps you've been part of a work team in which people think that the team's a good one: that is, people get on well with each other, the team's doing what's expected and so on. Many teams that I meet during my work in organisations on building high-performing teams think that they're already performing well, and I sense that some people are complacently thinking, 'We're okay, leave us alone!'

You certainly don't want to disrupt or undermine teamwork by questioning or challenging team members about how good the team is, but you may want your team to be more self-critical to achieve the following:

✔ Identify the team's strengths and ensure that the team is using those strengths fully.

✔ Clarify any weaknesses and work on overcoming them.

✔ Establish a mindset or culture of continuous improvement within the team.

Encourage members of your team to question whether, and to what extent, they focus on improving how the team functions by examining the agenda of team meetings with them and asking questions such as:

✔ Does the agenda focus solely on progressing the work and tasks we have to do, and on solving problems we're experiencing in getting our work done?

✔ Do any agenda items focus our attention on how well we're working and interacting as a team?

✔ How often do we spend time at the end of team meetings reviewing how effectively we've worked together during the meeting?

Separating the great from the good

Some teams display most – and a few great teams, all – of the characteristics of high performance. Have you ever experienced being a member of a great team (at work or socially) that you felt was extra-special? If so, complete the following short exercise so that you can better relate to the characteristics required for work teams to be great rather than just good. If not, take a look at the list of characteristics of a great team that I include after the exercise.

1. **Divide the pages of a notebook into three columns as in Table 11-1.**

2. **Write a brief description of the team that you think was a great team.**

3. **List the characteristics in the second column that separated this team – what made it great or extra-special – from other teams that you've been in.**

4. **Describe in the third column, if you can, the contribution that each characteristic made to building or sustaining teamwork.** You may have difficulty clearly describing the contribution that each characteristic made to teamwork, because good teamwork is often the product of an amalgam of characteristics.

5. **Repeat steps 2 to 4 for any other teams that you've been part of that you think were great or outstanding.**

I give an example in Table 11-1 of an outstanding work team and two characteristics of the team to help you get started.

Table 11-1	Examining Great Teams	
Brief Description of the Team	*Characteristics of the Team*	*Contribution Each Characteristic Made to Teamwork*
Team of analysts in an industrial chemistry laboratory	Took the initiative to help colleagues to complete their work	Reinforced strong relationships or bonds among team members
	Constructively challenged any behaviour that didn't fit with the team's work ethic	Promptly raising and quickly resolving issues that may undermine teamwork became the norm

If you're yet to work as part of a great team (and even if you have), the crucial aspect is that team members are effectively engaging each other. (Check out Chapters 5 and 6 for the importance of engagement and how to become an engaging leader.) Great teams have the following characteristics:

✔ **Shared sense of purpose.** The purpose is so strong and meaningful that team members put more, or at least as much, emphasis on achieving this purpose as on their own needs. (You find out more about team purpose in the later section 'Harnessing the power of team purpose'.)

✔ **Commitment to each other.** Team members look out for and look after one another; they're sensitive to how well others are coping with, for example, demanding workloads and support each other when necessary.

✔ **Openness and honesty.** Every member of the team expresses their views and opinions openly and honestly, and says what's on their mind. They can to do so because of the mutual trust and respect they have for one another.

✔ **Willingness to challenge each other as critical friends.** Team members question and challenge each others' views, ideas, opinions and proposals regarding team decisions, and when necessary, any attitudes or behaviours that don't meet the team's standards – and members accept being challenged themselves as a natural way of how the team works together.

✔ **Strong sense of team identity.** Team members have such a strong sense of connection that they strongly identify with their team and each other, and feel they're part of something special.

✔ **Mutual accountability.** Responsibility for holding team members accountable doesn't reside solely with the team leader. Every member of the team has and uses the right to hold each other accountable for upholding team standards and so on.

✔ **High performance and achievement.** The team is focused on the necessary objectives, results and/or targets, has a record for achieving outstanding performance and uses the other characteristics described in this list continually to question and challenge itself to improve its productivity.

Promote these characteristics in your team by making sure that you demonstrate the attitudes and behaviours that reflect these characteristics yourself. Providing a model of appropriate behaviour when you interact with other members of your team is a great way to lead and encourage team members to think, feel and act in the same ways.

Harnessing the power of team purpose

Why should members of your team get out of bed on a freezing winter morning and trudge through deep snow to come to work? If your answer is a simplistic 'because they're getting paid to do a job', you probably don't appreciate the importance of having a clear and compelling team purpose. (You can discover the value of a leader having clarity of purpose in Chapter 4.)

People want to contribute through the work they do:

✔ They want their work to have meaning – to be meaningful rather than be meaningless or pointless. (Chapter 5 describes how to avoid the 'black hole' of meaningless work.)

✔ They want to make a positive difference, for example, to the following:

- The success of their organisation.

- The lives of other people.

The power of having a clear and compelling team purpose is that it enables team members to contribute through:

✔ Having a clear focus.

✔ Harnessing their energy.

✔ Enabling every individual to express themselves.

✔ Using their talents, wisdom and expertise.

✔ Experiencing a sense of fulfilment through their contribution.

Involve members of your team in considering questions such as the following, and assimilating the answers to produce a simple, clear and concise statement of your team's purpose:

✔ What is our *raison d'être*? Why does this team exist?

✔ Who do we serve – who are our customers and stakeholders – and what do they expect from us?

- What is this team's unique contribution to making our organisation successful and/or achieving our organisation's (strategic) objectives?
- Where have we been and where are we going?
- What can we extract about the purpose of this team from documents such as strategic or business plans, department objectives/plans and so on?

Share your team's purpose with your customers and stakeholders – groups who are interested in and/or are affected by the work your team does – to test whether it resonates with them.

The purpose of your team needs to contribute to your organisation's mission statement, if it has produced one. Even without such a statement, use your team's purpose to check and ensure that your expected objectives are important and worthwhile: that working on achieving these items is contributing to the team achieving its purpose in the organisation and, through this, contributing to the success of the organisation.

You may have to go over this process several times to refine your team's purpose into a simple, clear and concise statement. Try the 'lift statement' test: is the description of your team's purpose so clear and concise that you can explain it to someone in a lift in the time the lift takes to travel five floors without stopping?

Invest time in clarifying and producing the team purpose, values and behaviours that together give your team its identity and have a unifying effect on it. You want to achieve the following:

- A purpose that unites everyone because people perceive the purpose to be so irresistible that it not only grabs and holds their attention, but they also feel compelled to contribute everything they can to achieving or delivering the purpose.
- Values and behaviours that are principles and reference points to guide how team members work together in achieving the team's purpose.

(You can find out how to clarify the purpose of your role and the objectives you have to achieve in Chapter 4. You may use the approach described there to involve your team in clarifying the team's objectives from the team's purpose.)

Valuing team values

Many teams are hindered in becoming high-performing teams because team members haven't clarified and agreed the values that are important to them and how they expect each other to behave vis-à-vis those values. (Chapter 3 has loads more information on why values need to underpin your leadership and how to clarify your own values.)

Holding a meeting with team members to clarify the values that are important to your team enables you and them to do the following:

- ✔ Get to know each other better by talking about each person's important values.

- ✔ Practise being open and honest with each other through revealing personal values.

- ✔ Experience reconciling differences by having meaningful conversations with each other.

- ✔ Set standards of behaviour for how team members treat each other and work together.

- ✔ Use the agreed values and behaviours to improve teamwork by recognising and reinforcing good behaviour, and challenging anyone whose behaviour may undermine, or is undermining, how the team performs. (You can find out in Chapter 8 how delaying tackling under-performance may cause the 'bad apple' effect: when a person's unacceptable performance or behaviour affects his work colleagues.)

Try the following exercise with your team:

1. **Organise a meeting with your team so that you're not disturbed for at least two hours.**

2. **Explain how values and behaviours are important to how team members work together.**

Hanging on and stopping back

I worked with a company's senior management team to build a high-performance culture, initially through building a high-performing management team that would be a role model for managers who reported to it and their employees. The management team held a three-hour meeting to share, explore and agree the values that were important to how members of the team worked together and how senior managers expected team members to behave to reinforce those agreed values.

Two of the team's agreed values and examples of relevant behaviour were as follows:

✔ **We value individual creativity and independence of thought.** We fully consider new ideas and concepts, and don't dismiss or ridicule them because they challenge the norm.

✔ **We value high levels of trust among team members.** We display integrity and consistency in our discussions and actions. We don't criticise team members to other employees.

At the end of regular team meetings, the team used these values and behaviours as reference points to discuss and examine how well they were working together. They also agreed to 'hang on and stop back' after certain meetings that involved more junior managers and employees, in order to discuss how team members had reinforced or undermined the agreed values in working with those managers and employees.

3. **Ask each team member to write down, without conferring, a list of the values that he thinks the team should have to enable members of the team to work effectively together.** You may need to give an example of what you mean by a value, such as 'being open and honest'. If you have a large team, form sub-groups of two to three people to produce the initial list.

4. **Share and discuss the lists identifying where values are the same or similar, and exploring the differences with the aim of agreeing the values that the team will adopt.**

5. **Take each agreed value in turn and identify and agree two or three behaviours that demonstrate that a team member is working in accord with the value.** Examples of behaviours for 'open and honest' may be:

   - All team members say what's 'on their mind'.

   - We encourage team members to express their point of view.

6. **Discuss and agree how the team are going to use the agreed list of values, and review how well every team member is acting and behaving in accord with these values.**

The following are ways of using the agreed values and behaviours:

✔ Displaying the list of values and behaviours in your team's work area.

✔ Discussing how well members of the team are working in accord with the agreed values and behaviours at the end of whole-team and sub-team meetings.

✔ Examining during one-to-one performance and capability appraisals how well each team member is putting the values into practice in working with colleagues.

Assessing the Effectiveness of Your Team

Assessing just how effectively your team is performing enables you to understand the team's strengths and the priorities to work on to improve its performance. You may have heard the adage 'what get's measured, get's done', and perhaps even already use this approach to focus team members on the team's expected targets and to know how well the team is performing. If not, consider how you can best adopt the approaches described in the following two sections to assess and improve your team's performance.

Rating your team

No doubt you have a view about how well your team's performing. This view is based on, or coloured by, a mixture of your experiences of working with individual team members and the whole team, the range of problems being encountered, the output from your team and so on.

A subjective, instinctive idea is fine, but adopting a more structured approach to considering your team's performance allows you to be more objective and thus produce a more accurate assessment to rating your team.

You can assess how effectively your team is performing against several criteria including:

✔ How well your team is achieving its objectives, targets and/or results, sometimes referred to as key performance indicators (KPIs).

✔ The extent to which team members are working in accord with the team's agreed values and behaviours. (You can discover how to clarify and agree team values and behaviours with your team in the earlier section 'Valuing team values'.)

✔ Whether the team has the characteristics that you consider are important for your team. Take a look at the earlier section 'Separating the great from the good', in which I list the key characteristics of a great team or, indeed, you identified yourself by completing the exercise.

To rate your team, book time with yourself on a regular basis and ask yourself questions such as the following:

✔ How well is my team performing against the KPIs – the objectives/targets/results – that we have to achieve? What numeric or other evidence can I use to justify my view?

✔ Has my team's performance in achieving our KPIs been steady, improved or deteriorated over the preceding one and three months? What are the reasons for any changes in performance trends?

- How well are team members working together? What have I noticed about how team members are behaving and treating each other that supports my view?

- How well do team members support each other? What evidence exists that team members are on the 'look out' for how others are coping with the workload, and are taking the initiative to help each other when they see someone struggling?

- Do team members hold each other accountable for doing what they expect each other to do? To what extent do team members promptly challenge their colleagues when they don't do what's expected?

- What evidence can I find that team members, individually and collectively, are interacting and behaving in ways that reinforce our team values? What have I done since my last review to recognise and reinforce good practice? How promptly and effectively have I intervened when I notice unacceptable behaviour and standards of work?

- On a scale of 1–10, what's my rating of the team atmosphere as a happy productive place to be? What is the evidence on which I have based my score? How does my score compare with previous scores? What actions am I going to take to improve the team atmosphere?

You can use any characteristics that you want your team to have in a simple questionnaire to rate your team.

Conducting a team self-assessment

No, I'm not suggesting that you buy a baton and wave your arms around maniacally like an orchestral maestro! I have something a little more collaborative in mind. Carrying out regular self-assessments of your team's performance allows you to develop an overview of how well your team's performing, especially if you hold regular reviews and look for trends in performance. Such self-assessments have the following benefits:

✔ You can reinforce KPIs, values and behaviours, and important team characteristics by using them as criteria for conducting the assessment.

✔ Team members are more likely to take ownership of the outcomes of the assessment because they've been involved in assessing their team.

✔ All team members contribute to establishing a culture of continuous improvement through regularly critiquing the team's performance. (You find out more on this subject in the later section 'Striving for Continuous Improvement'.)

Hold a team meeting to describe the reasons why you want your team to conduct a self-assessment, and the method that you're going to use, before you ask team members to assess or comment on the team's performance. Then involve team members in assessing how well their team is performing by:

✔ Examining the productivity of the team using numeric performance information, graphs showing performance trends, progress in completing projects and so on.

✔ Asking questions such as those described in the previous section 'Rating your team'.

Consider whether all team members are likely to give an honest, objective and unbiased rating of team performance during a meeting. If you think that their colleagues' views may influence how some team members rate their team in an open discussion, collect everyone's assessment anonymously first via a questionnaire and then discuss the summary of those views.

Produce a simple questionnaire containing a description of the characteristics or issues that you want members of your team to consider, together with a simple rating scheme. Table 11-2 provides examples of statements that you may want to include in a questionnaire.

Table 11-2	Examples of Statements to Use in a Team Self-assessment			
	Strongly Disagree	*Tend to Disagree*	*Tend to Agree*	*Strongly Agree*
Everyone is encouraged to express their views and opinions openly and honestly.				
Team members hold each other accountable for doing what they say they're going to do.				
Everyone strives to uphold the team's values through their actions and behaviour.				
Team members challenge colleagues whose work, attitude and/or behaviour is below the team's standards.				
We regularly question all aspects of our work to identify our strengths and focus on continuously improving the team's performance.				
I'm proud to be a member of this team.				

Striving for Continuous Improvement

If your team is already performing well, why strive to improve performance continuously? Simply, for the following reasons:

✔ Continuous improvement is more of a 'team mindset' or team culture – a way of working – than a set of techniques or methods.

✔ Teams are never standing still; their performance is improving, or deteriorating due to complacency over time.

Building your team into a high-performing team and sustaining that high performance is difficult: a large majority of your team, if not every team member, needs to be committed to the team's purpose, upholding the team's values and beliefs, and maintaining high standards in all aspects of their work and how team members work together. The task isn't easy but is worthwhile. (Refer to the characteristics of high-performing teams in the earlier section 'Separating the great from the good' to gain insights into the benefits of high-performing teams.)

The enemy of continuous improvement is thinking that you're too busy actually getting the work done to spend time on improving how members of your team work together to get the work done!

Developing a high-performance atmosphere

You've probably walked into some organisations and sensed a real 'buzz' about the place; high energy, employees really engaged in their work and enjoying themselves, an 'air' of professionalism and high productivity, and so on. You may also have experienced walking into certain shops, hotels, restaurants and so on and sensed an air of stagnation or lethargy!

The tone or mood – the atmosphere – in a workplace is partly created by the physical environment, but primarily by the people who work there. I've come across workplaces that are cathedrals of modern architecture and ergonomics but void of purposefulness and spirit.

Try to provide the best facilities, tools and equipment for your team to be productive, *and* focus most of your effort on the human aspects of work to create a high-performance atmosphere.

Work on creating a high-performance team atmosphere as follows:

- ✔ Share your vision of how you see your team performing as a high- performing team. (Dip into Chapter 4 to find out how to create your own vision.)

- ✔ Regularly reinforce the team's purpose and *raison d'être*, as well as the contribution that the team is making to the organisation's success, in team meetings and conversations with individuals and groups. (Discover how to clarify your team's purpose in the earlier section 'Harnessing the power of team purpose'.)

- ✔ Display the team's achievements around the workplace. Use graphs or other means of showing statistical trends in performance, feedback from customers and colleagues and so on.

- ✔ Catch people doing great deeds; get out of your office and walk around looking for examples of people doing a great job.

- ✔ Ensure that enough priority and time is given to activities focused on critically examining how well the team is performing and how well people are working together to identify strengths and agree actions to improve all aspects of team performance.

- ✔ Encourage people to seize opportunities to get to know each other better, such as talking about who they are, their hopes and aspirations, the challenges they face and so on.

- ✔ Celebrate the achievement of significant objectives and targets, passing important milestones in improving productivity and so on by organising an event for people to have fun, enjoy being together and (informally) tell stories about their achievements.

Making the un-discussable discussable

Have you ever experienced colleagues sharing their views and opinions with you after a meeting that, in your view, they should have said during the meeting? In my experience, people aren't open and honest in expressing their views in meetings for the following reasons (among others):

- They're concerned about appearing ignorant or foolish by expressing their views or opinions.

- They don't want to feel embarrassed by saying something inappropriate.

- They don't want to embarrass or hurt a work colleague by disagreeing with or criticising that person's view or opinion.

- They lack the confidence to make a statement that they can't prove or validate.

- They're concerned about how a colleague may react – even overreact – if that person disagrees with the view and proceeds to criticise their personality as well as their viewpoint.

Being open and honest in meetings by 'speaking your mind' is risky for many people; they have to step outside of their comfort zone to be able to take the risk. (Explore Chapter 2 to find out more about comfort zones and Chapter 6 to discover lots of good practice on how to have meaningful conversations with your staff.)

Here are some approaches to make the un-discussable discussable in team meetings:

- Encourage your team members to question and challenge your views, and listen attentively to their views and opinions. (Refer to Chapter 6 to find out how to invite challenge and cope with embarrassment and threat.) Adopting this approach allows you to set a great example for others to copy.

- Have a brief chat before a meeting with a person who you know lacks confidence to speak in meetings. Discuss agenda items that are important to that person and encourage him to express his views in the meeting: say that you'll support his viewpoint if you agree with it, especially if you expect people to have different views on the agenda item.

- Invite more introverted individuals to speak by using their name and ensuring that colleagues don't interrupt.

- Challenge (constructively) any language or behaviour that's likely to cause embarrassment, threat or undermine anyone's self-confidence.

✔ Recognise and praise individuals who ask searching questions that cause their colleagues, and even the whole team, to question existing viewpoints and lead to new insights, enhanced understanding of problems and improved decision-making. (Find out how to become more skilled in asking searching questions in Chapter 6.)

✔ Thank in private a team member who constructively challenges a colleague's unacceptable behaviour, such as regularly interrupting and 'talking over' other colleagues while they're expressing their views.

Chapter 12

Leading Your Senior Management Team

. . . .

In This Chapter

▶ Building collective responsibility

▶ Coping with increasing pressure and complexity

▶ Developing a senior management team to be proud of

▶ Creating time for your strategic priorities

. . . .

*Y*ou probably think that when you've made it to the top and are leading your organisation's senior management team, many of the earlier problems you experienced in leading teams are behind you. Surely, you can now expect your team to be highly committed and competent team players. After all, they have loads of experience of participating in and leading their own teams, and must have learnt from their experiences.

In fact, leading a top team can be more demanding and challenging than leading other types of team, as you discover in this chapter. You explore a range of challenges that you may experience, and find out how to build a high-performing team of responsible senior managers by using and enhancing their talents.

Developing a Collective Sense of Responsibility

This section takes a look at two common problems that you can come up against when leading a senior management team:

✔ Managers becoming too dependent on you when you exert too much control.

✔ Managers developing too narrow a viewpoint at the expense of the organisation as a whole.

Breaking the dependency cycle

Most Managing Directors (MD) and Chief Executives are, in my experience, focused on results. They expect their senior managers to achieve high results and act with a sense of urgency. Such expectations – and how an MD typically behaves as a consequence – can create a *dependency cycle* as follows:

1. The MD is impatient to see results and perceives that things are moving too slowly.

2. She therefore leaps in and instructs senior managers what to do.

3. The managers infer that the MD wants total control and so begin to wait for the intervention each time. They become dependent on the MD to make decisions.

4. The MD's frustrations grow at the lack of senior managerial input; she jumps in even earlier and the managers back off even more.

5. The dependency cycle continues.

Constantly taking control of situations and telling people what you want them to do encourages them to stop thinking for themselves and wait, or ask, for direction: even for instructions! Just like John in the sidebar 'Avoiding the Dependency Cycle', you have to be aware that your behaviour may have unintended consequences in that you can contribute to creating what you consider to be unacceptable behaviour in others.

Effectively changing the behaviour of your managers may well need to start with you managing changes in your own behaviour. Before you can change any aspect of your behaviour regarding, for example, how you interact with your managers, you have to:

Avoiding the dependency cycle

John was Managing Director of a large manufacturing company. When I started working with him and his senior management team, I realised quickly that John was highly results driven. For example, he expected management meetings to be productive: managers were expected to quickly get to the bottom of problems, make decisions, agree actions and deadlines for taking them, and (subsequently) hold each other accountable for taking action.

John became frustrated with what he saw as the managers' slow progress in management meetings. So he stepped in, made decisions and told managers what he wanted them to do. Managers interpreted that he wanted to make all the main decisions, and so they let John take over the meetings.

John's increasing frustration at the 'inertia' among his managers caused him to step in sooner, which caused them to wait for him to do so. Hence, the dependency cycle was established as John's managers became more dependent on him for making decisions.

I coached John to manage his frustrations and actively engage his managers in collective decision-making, while simultaneously coaching managers to encourage them and build their confidence to contribute more to meetings to break the cycle.

- ✔ Become aware of the behaviour.
- ✔ Recognise the effects and consequences of that behaviour on others.
- ✔ Accept that your behaviour isn't having the desired effect on your colleagues.
- ✔ Want to change your behaviour.

Continually work on developing members of your management team to contribute fully to making decisions by:

- ✔ Being aware of your behaviour and its potential effects on your managers. (Dip into Chapter 2 to find out more about how to become more aware of your behaviour and how it affects others.)

- ✔ Encouraging each of your managers to give you honest feedback about how your behaviour affects them.

- ✔ Developing and modelling the behaviour you expect from others. (You can find more about being a great role model in Chapter 8.)

- ✔ Creating space for and encouraging your managers to express themselves by not dominating or smothering them in management meetings.

Helping managers out of their silos

You've probably noticed grain silos – tall, narrow, bullet-shaped structures – in the countryside, but what are *management silos*? Well, these silos exist when managers become totally focused on their department and achieving their department objectives and targets: they develop a narrow focus – hence the notion of silos – instead of taking a broad, whole-business perspective.

As I describe in Chapter 10, 'what gets measured, gets done'! This notion is often a significant factor in creating management silos, especially because many businesses and other organisations have invested a lot of time and effort in developing *key performance indicators* (KPIs) to measure how well departments and the overall business is performing.

Robustly holding managers accountable for achieving their KPIs can have the unintended consequence of creating management silos in which your managers work independently, rather than interdependently, and rely on you to resolve issues and problems between departments.

The following actions can help managers to escape from their silos:

- ✔ Checking that the KPIs that the company is using are complementary and reinforcing the success of the whole business/organisation. Identify any departmental KPIs that may cause tensions between departments/managers. One example is achieving sales targets and effective production efficiency in a manufacturing business: the sales department may accept orders that have to be delivered by a certain deadline to hit their sales KPIs, which causes problems for production because their schedules have to be changed in ways that lower production efficiency.

✔ Facilitating dialogue between managers to examine how well departments are achieving KPIs, and exploring any negative effects of any manager's actions to achieve their KPIs on other managers.

✔ Encouraging managers to take collective responsibility for the success of the whole organisation as well as the success of their department.

Encouraging Courageous Conversations

The work of senior management teams is, in my experience, becoming more demanding, complex and difficult, especially with regard to anticipating potential issues, understanding and solving problems, and making the right decisions. Most management teams have to wrestle with, at least some of, the following challenges:

✔ Customers are becoming more demanding, often wanting 'more for less'!

✔ Competition is increasing as businesses compete with global rather than local competitors.

✔ Advances in information technology are creating expectations of immediate access to people, fast responses to messages and so on.

✔ Organisations are becoming more complex to manage due to the increasing use of matrix structures, project and virtual teams and the advance of globalisation.

The cumulative effect of these changes may be that you and your managers experience increasing pressure to achieve results and improve performance. This pressure can result in individual managers becoming too narrowly focused and may fragment teamwork if managers become critical of other departments or colleagues who (they think) are behaving in ways that are adversely affecting the operation or performance of their own department.

An important part of your role as the most senior manager is to encourage and help your managers to engage each other effectively and build teamwork, especially when your team comprises strong characters who may hold significantly different views and opinions. Therefore, effective communication on the part of all managers is vital.

Keeping your managers' heads up

Encouraging your managers to have courageous conversations doesn't mean that they're allowed to have arguments and go into battle with each other! It does mean encouraging them to say what needs to be said to address challenges and get to the bottom of, and solve, problems. A critical factor that affects whether managers express their views is whether they fear they're going to get their head chopped off!

You – and anyone in your management team – chop colleagues' heads off when you:

- ✔ Reject their view or opinion outright without an explanation.
- ✔ Ridicule their view or opinion.
- ✔ Embarrass them in public by saying things such as, 'You should have known better.'

Encourage your managers to have courageous conversations in which they:

- ✔ Speak their mind.
- ✔ Listen attentively to each other.
- ✔ Question and challenge each others' thinking with the intention of enhancing collective understanding and making better decisions.
- ✔ Don't cut each other off when they're speaking.
- ✔ Stop intentionally ridiculing or embarrassing their colleagues.

The next section 'Critiquing each other's thoughts and ideas' contains more on challenging others' thinking. (Also, check out Chapter 5 for ways to engage colleagues effectively in meaningful conversations.)

Critiquing each other's thoughts and ideas

Have you noticed how you sometimes become attached to your thoughts? If so, you've probably felt that someone was criticising you when they questioned or challenged your idea, view, suggestion or proposal.

As senior management problems become more complex, so problem-solving becomes more complex. I suggest that the possibility of one manager knowing the best solution to a complex problem is highly unlikely. The best solution is much more likely to evolve out of a dialogue between managers, in which they enhance each others' understanding and come to a shared understanding of the problem; and, in doing so, establish a common commitment to take action.

Critiquing your colleagues' thoughts is an important aspect of enhancing understanding because:

✔ The validity of the individual's thought or view is tested.

✔ Any assumptions on which the thought or view is based can be revealed and their validity tested.

✔ Managers may be prompted to expand on, and even clarify, their own views as well as contribute to other people's thinking.

Help your managers to realise and accept that they're not their thoughts! By accepting this notion, your managers are more likely to:

✔ Keep an open mind to enable the best solution to evolve.

✔ Be willing to critique each other's thinking.

✔ Be receptive to having their colleagues question and critique their ideas, views and opinions.

Being strong by being vulnerable

Many managers that I've met seem to think that being strong means strongly articulating their views, projecting themselves in ways that have a big impact and influence on their colleagues.

Such management behaviour can be perceived to be domineering by some, perhaps more introverted, managers who may find it difficult to question or challenge the views of their more outspoken colleagues.

A manager may be having an unhealthy influence on decision-making in your management team if colleagues have difficulty questioning and challenging that person's views.

Take the lead in encouraging everyone in your management team to question and challenge each other's thinking and/or unacceptable behaviour:

✔ Set an example through asking searching questions of your managers to clarify their thinking and express their views clearly and concisely. (Read Chapter 6 to discover how to develop your ability to ask searching questions.)

✔ Invite and encourage your managers to point out to you any aspect of your behaviour that discourages them from expressing their views and/or questioning your views. (Dip into Chapter 6 to discover how to invite your managers to challenge you, and how to cope with embarrassment.) Read the sidebar 'Let me have it!' to find out how one Managing Director encouraged his managers to challenge his unacceptable behaviour.

✔ Constructively challenge any manager whose behaviour is adversely affecting colleagues contributing to decision-making.

Let me have it!

Neville, a Managing Director of a large engineering company, is a strong character who has a big influence on his management team. When I started working with Neville and his management team, I soon discovered that at times Neville dominated his managers.

As part of our work on improving the performance of the senior management team and the company, Neville and his team clarified the values that were important to how they worked as a team, and the associated behaviours that they expected of each other. Neville and his managers agreed to use the values and behaviours as criteria to assess informally how they were contributing to meetings, and provide feedback to each other at the end of certain meetings on how individual managers had reinforced or undermined the values through how they behaved in the meeting.

Neville noticed that managers were providing useful feedback to each other, but some seemed reluctant to give him feedback that was critical of his behaviour. He encouraged everyone to critique his behaviour by naming managers who were giving him useful feedback, even if it was in private, providing examples of the feedback, and how he valued their honesty. He explained that he was experiencing difficulty in changing aspects of his behaviour that were the habits of a lifetime, and he encouraged all his managers to continue giving him feedback about how his behaviour was reinforcing and/or undermining the team's values.

Neville still has a big influence on his team, but he now engages and empowers managers to make a greater contribution to the team.

Sharing Accountability for Success

As head of your organisation you may sense that your managers think that the 'buck stops with you' because you're ultimately responsible and accountable for everything. The potential problem for you with this mindset is that they look to you to sort out most, if not all, things regarding the performance of your management team, instead of sharing accountability with you for how well team members work together.

One way to see whether your managers hold this unhelpful view is to test whether they share accountability with you for ensuring that management meetings are effective.

Reflect on how your managers typically act in meetings and tick one of the boxes for each of the statements listed in Table 12-1.

Table 12-1	Testing Your Managers' Accountability in Meetings			
	Never	**Rarely**	**Often**	**Always**
1. Managers promptly point out when time is being wasted by people going off on a tangent, into too much detail and so on.				
2. Managers promptly and constructively challenge any colleague whose behaviour is inappropriate.				
3. Managers look to me to ensure that each meeting is productive.				
4. Managers look to me to ensure that people work well together.				

If you ticked one of the first two columns in rows 1 and 2, and one of the last two columns in rows 3 and 4, your managers probably don't share accountability for the success of their management meetings with you. Think about any implications of your rating: if your managers don't share accountability for the effectiveness of their management meetings, what do they share accountability for?

The next three sections show you how to encourage and establish shared accountability among your managers.

Stopping the blame game

One of the most damaging things you and your managers can do is to kill a sense of shared accountability by blaming a colleague, regardless of whether that person caused the problem or not. In my experience, some managers are overly critical of colleagues in a negative, even derogatory, way; as if deliberately trying to embarrass the colleague or show the person in a 'bad light'. The intentions behind such behaviour aren't positive or constructive if the manager is:

- ✔ Projecting blame onto a colleague to keep themselves out of the spotlight when the cause of the problem is unclear.

- ✔ Promoting themselves at the expense of their colleague.

- ✔ Undermining their colleague's self-confidence or self-esteem.

Far better is to promote positive attitudes and behaviour in your team as follows:

- ✔ Promote the behaviour that you and managers expect of each other by agreeing the team's values, and associated behaviours. (You can discover how to involve team members in clarifying and agreeing team values and behaviours in Chapter 11.)

- ✔ Encourage managers to give feedback to each other at the end of team meetings on how well they're upholding the agreed values and behaviours.

- ✔ Explain the consequences of unacceptable behaviour on the performance of the team.

- ✔ Describe to a manager who behaves in an unacceptable way how you feel about her behaviour, and also describe the changes that you expect the manager to make.

Creating a healthy environment

You may be wondering what a healthy (senior management) team environment is or looks like! Such an environment is one in which:

- ✔ All managers are actively taking and sharing accountability for the success of the team and how it's performing.

- ✔ A real 'buzz' is present: a sense of high positive energy. (Dip into Chapter 11 to discover how to create a high-performance atmosphere.)

- ✔ Everyone is totally engaged, and engaging each other, in striving to achieve and improve performance.

- ✔ A strong sense of camaraderie is evident based on trust and mutual respect, and managers have a genuine interest in each other. (Drop into Chapter 6 to find more on having a genuine interest in others.)

✔ Occasional tension exists between team members because sharing different perspectives, views and preferences is seen as natural, and expressing and challenging differences is used constructively to improve understanding of problems and issues, and make better decisions.

✔ Managers are learning from and with each other, and developing their skills and abilities together.

Strive to establish and sustain a healthy environment in which everyone is collectively responsible and sharing accountability for optimising team performance by behaving as follows:

✔ Be enthusiastic and positive about:

- Your team's purpose; its *raison d'être*.

- The objectives and targets you want your team to achieve.

- Your vision for the organisation. (Refer to Chapter 4 to find out how to develop a sense of purpose and create your own vision.)

✔ Set high standards of behaviour and performance, and encourage your managers to meet them.

✔ Coach your managers to become skilled in engaging each other. (Find out how to become an engaging leader in Chapter 6, and discover more about coaching in Chapter 8.)

✔ Conduct team self-assessments to identify and build on your team's strengths, and involve all your team in continually improving its performance. (Flip to Chapter 11 to discover how to conduct team assessments.)

✔ Consider the value of using a highly skilled independent coach and facilitator to support you to accelerate establishing shared accountability within your team. If you're wondering what to look for in a good independent coach/facilitator and how to select one, I suggest that the person:

- Displays integrity, self-confidence and humility.

- Is skilled in quickly building trust and respect with and between all managers.

- Fully engages everyone in the team in working on improving how the team works.

- Constructively challenges and supports individuals and the whole team to be the best they can be.

- Demonstrates high personal and ethical standards.

✔ Ask a coach/facilitator for:

- Examples of how she has worked with senior management teams.

- Challenges she has faced in working with senior management teams and how she overcame them.

- References for you to contact to discuss how she works with teams and the value of her work.

Embedding the behaviours you cherish

Your senior management team should be a microcosm of the organisation you aspire to create because:

✔ Your senior management team (or, better still, your senior leadership team) is a role model for the rest of your organisation. (Chapter 8 describes how to become a great role model.)

✔ Leading a change in attitudes and behaviour – a change in culture – within your organisation starts at the top.

Old habits die hard! Managers can easily slip back into old behaviours and ways of working if you don't continually promote and reinforce the attitudes and behaviours you cherish until those attitudes and behaviours become the norm.

Here's how to embed those desired attitudes and behaviours:

✔ Be the person that you want others to become; promote through your own actions the attitude and behaviours that you expect from others.

✔ Catch your managers demonstrating the right attitudes and behaviours. Look for, recognise and praise 'in public' individuals who are demonstrating the right behaviour; noticing and talking only about what managers are doing wrong is all too easy!

✔ Tell stories of great examples of managers demonstrating the behaviours you cherish, and how those managers have contributed to the success of your organisation. (Find out about the power of story-telling in Chapter 10.)

✔ Promote managers who demonstrate the right attitudes and behaviours to reinforce to everyone that people who think and act in these ways are more likely to be promoted.

Preparing Others for Leadership

You need leaders throughout your organisation because employees' immediate line manager exerts the biggest influence on the extent to which employees are engaged in their work and committed to doing their job to the best of their ability. Some organisations adopt a structured approach to developing leaders that may include:

✔ Assessing individual competence against clearly defined leadership competences within appraisal or performance and development reviews, and planning how to develop leaders' competences.

✔ Having succession plans for key leadership positions within the organisation, and using career development to develop individuals to be ready to step into those positions.

✔ Coaching leaders to improve their performance within their current role and/or to head up business improvement projects.

✔ Secondments into a range of leadership positions in the organisation to enable individuals to:

- Develop their leadership skills through being exposed to different challenges and problems.

- Acquire knowledge and a good understanding of the organisation/business and how it functions.

Put 'leadership' onto the agenda of your key management meetings and ensure that you and your senior management team regularly discuss the quality of leadership in your organisation and how to develop great leaders.

Spotting potential high flyers

You can adopt a structured approach to spotting and developing potential high flyers by using some of or all the methods described in the preceding section. Another approach is to get around your organisation and notice the potential high flyers doing great work. You can discover a lot about your organisation as well as your people by coming out from behind your desk and informally talking to people in their workplace. Ask people about their:

✔ Hopes and aspirations for the organisation and themselves.

✔ Frustrations and concerns about what is or isn't happening in the workplace.

✔ Ideas and suggestions about how to improve any aspect of the operation or functioning of the organisation.

Spot potential high flyers by:

✔ Wandering around your organisation and chatting to your people to get to know them and your organisation better.

✔ Being clear about the attributes, characteristics and/or competences that you're looking for in a leader so that you're better able to spot them. You may be looking for individuals who:

- Are 'standard-bearers' by promoting and achieving particularly high standards in their work area.

- Have a track record of achieving very high levels of performance.

- Are constructively critical of sub-standard work and service wherever it occurs or is produced, and take the initiative to try to influence the relevant people to take action to improve performance.

✔ Talking to employees about whether they want to be involved in making improvements that they'd like to see in the organisation. Would you see leadership potential in someone who's critical about an aspect of how the organisation's working, but doesn't want to get involved in making improvements? I wouldn't!

Working yourself out of a job

Do you – like too many MDs and other senior managers – do work that you shouldn't be doing? Do you make decisions that your managers can be making? If you plead 'guilty as charged' to these questions, be aware that managers may be working at levels below what they're being paid for throughout your organisation, because such behaviour tends to cascade down and through each management level.

You may think that I'm crazy for saying this, but I suggest that you work yourself out of your job rather than do the work of managers that report to you.

When you're doing most of the thinking and telling your managers what you want them to do, you're conditioning your managers to follow instructions: this behaviour contributes to creating the dependency that I describe in the earlier section 'Breaking the Dependency Cycle'. Engaging your managers fully in making decisions encourages them to think and learn, individually and collectively, how to solve complex and difficult problems so that they can eventually make such decisions themselves without involving you. Some individuals may eventually demonstrate that they're capable of stepping into your shoes!

Work yourself out of your job as follows:

- ✔ Hold yourself back from stepping down and making decisions for your managers. (Dip into the section 'Breaking the Dependency Cycle' earlier in this chapter for tips on how to avoid taking control.)

- ✔ Describe and show your commitment to developing your management team – and your organisation – to achieve results now and build capability to sustain success in the future.

- ✔ Encourage your managers to be collectively responsible and share accountability for the performance of your team and the results you expect them to achieve. (You can find out how to encourage your managers to share accountability in the earlier section 'Sharing Accountability for Success'.)

- ✔ Delegate tasks to your managers as they become more competent in order to free you up to concentrate on your strategic priorities.

Part V
The Part of Tens

"It's just one meeting after another."

In this part . . .

*T*hese short chapters are packed with tips on good leadership practice. You can find inspiration here on how to take the lead and lead others.

Chapter 13

Ten Tips on Taking the Lead

● ●

In This Chapter

▶ Knowing the real you

▶ Being a positive leader

▶ Becoming more influential

● ●

*B*oundless opportunities are available for you to take the lead in all sorts of situations, if you're willing to step forward and have a positive influence and impact on the people who work for and with you. This chapter contains ten tips to help you step up and lead in ways to ensure that people accept you taking the initiative.

Making Leadership Common Sense Your Common Practice

Leadership can be challenging because you have to consider so many things when leading people in a work environment including the following:

▶ The business's needs.

▶ People's different and varying needs and expectations.

▶ Demands on you to deliver results.

▶ Your boss's, your own and work colleagues' priorities.

You may have difficulty reconciling all the different expectations that people have of you, including your own expectation of yourself.

I encourage you to use your common sense and do what you think is right in every situation, especially when you feel that you're in a dilemma. Yes, you have to be able to justify your decisions to others, but you also have to justify your decisions to yourself: you have to live with your decisions. You can't please all the people all the time and, fortunately for you and all leaders, leading people isn't a popularity contest!

All anyone, including yourself, can ask of you in any situation is to act with integrity and make the best decision you can with the information you have by using your common sense.

Leading Yourself First

You may be asking 'why do I need to think about leading myself when leadership is about leading other people?'. The reason is because you have a big impact on the people who work for and with you!

Knowing your motives and values, being aware of how you feel – your emotional state – at any time, and having a good understanding of how these things affect the way you think and act enables you to appreciate how your emotional state and behaviour can impact on colleagues. (Chapter 2 contains useful info on increasing self-knowledge through self-questioning, and obtaining feedback from people about how your behaviour is affecting them.)

Good self-knowledge and personal insight enables you to consider and choose the best approaches to working with people, approaches that have the desired effect on people and achieve your objectives.

Being Authentic

I believe that leaders have to live with themselves before they can live with anyone else. Leaders must to be true to their core values and beliefs.

Perhaps you've experienced at least one occasion when you were in a dilemma and uncertain about what to do: you made a decision only to find that you had doubts about whether it was right or not; or perhaps you even experienced those doubts gnawing away at your conscience. I suspect that these feelings indicate that the decision you made didn't fit with your values.

Be authentic and act in accord with your core values. Your colleagues appreciate when you do so and act with integrity, even if they don't always agree with your decisions. (Chapter 2 contains more on being an authentic leader.)

Being a Healthy (Self) Critic

One of the most powerful ways of becoming a better leader is to learn from your experiences. Make a point of noticing when you do something really well as a leader and store the lesson away for future use. Similarly, remember when you make a bad mistake and resolve not to do it again. Developing your leadership abilities through trial and error is a long, slow and potentially painful process.

You can accelerate the improvement of your leadership skills by optimising the way you learn from your experiences. Check out Chapter 2 for how to adopt a healthy approach to being self-critical and for more on taking lessons from your experiences.

One simple way to speed up becoming the leader you aspire to be is to spend a little time every day reflecting on what you did well and what you could have done better during that day.

Avoiding Being a Busy Fool

Almost without exception, every manager I've worked with says that they're very busy; probably the majority also say that they're overworked! Being busy and highly productive is admirable, but being busy and misusing or wasting time because you're not spending the right time on the right priorities to be successful is not.

Spending enough time on the right priorities requires you to prioritise effectively. Your team expect you to know and share your priorities with them: they probably also expect you to give them a sense of purpose and clear direction.

Use some of your time to become absolutely clear about your own and your team's purpose, and the objectives required to optimise your contribution to the organisation's success. Share this purpose with your staff and anyone else who may benefit from being clear about your team's role. (Chapter 4 contains advice on clarifying and achieving your priorities.)

Listening Before You Leap

You're no doubt familiar with the phrase 'fools rush in'. Be aware that you can act in too much haste when you're under pressure to solve a problem that (you think) has been caused by a colleague doing a job wrong, especially when you're up against a tight deadline.

If you're not careful, you can end up making a problem worse because you act before you've obtained, and fully understand, all the relevant information. Remember that you may wrongly or overly criticise a person who you believe has done their job wrong if you take this approach.

Although you use your ears for hearing, you use your mind for listening. To really listen to what someone's saying, you have to focus your close attention on that person. Talk and listen attentively to a person who you think has caused a problem by doing their job wrong especially whenever you feel under pressure to act. (Chapter 5 guides you in how to switch on your senses.)

'Working With' People Rather Than 'Doing To' People

Many leaders take the responsibility off the people who work for them in one of two ways: they're control freaks or too helpful. I describe their behaviour as 'doing to rather than working with' people as follows:

- Control freaks keep a close eye on what people are doing and refuse to delegate because they like to ensure that everything is correct: they trust only themselves!

✔ Overly helpful leaders tend to give detailed instructions about how to do a task, take problems off people and solve dilemmas for them.

Both groups often don't realise the unintended consequences of their behaviour, because being overly controlling or overly helpful causes problems. People can't develop their skills and confidence when you don't give them responsibility, don't trust them to do a job or don't allow them to think for themselves.

Encourage and enable people to learn to think for themselves when you're working with them, not least because your own job becomes easier when everyone who works for you is confident and competent in their job. (You find out how to really engage people in Chapter 6.)

Being Uncomfortably Comfortable

Taking the lead often requires you to get out of your comfort zone because you have to deal with situations, problems and dilemmas that you've never encountered before, and you're probably unsure about how to deal with them. Straying out of your comfort zone is risky because you expose yourself to potential failure and embarrassment if things don't go as well as you hope.

Develop a mentality of being 'uncomfortably comfortable' and enhance your self-confidence, so that you're okay operating outside of your comfort zone and promptly tackle problems and dilemmas. See problems as opportunities for you to test out your leadership skills, and learn from your successes and failures. Chapter 2 contains information on developing your self-confidence and covers expanding your comfort zone.

Speaking Up and Speaking Out!

An old Geordie saying says: 'Shy bairns get nowt!'. It literally means 'shy children get nothing', but is used to emphasise that people should speak up for themselves. I think that this saying applies to leaders.

Managers of virtually every team I've worked with have told me that they want their colleagues to speak openly and honestly in team meetings: they expect their colleagues to speak up and express their views and opinions. Speaking openly and honestly in management meetings is, however, in my experience easier said than done!

I'm not suggesting that managers are being dishonest with their colleagues; they may just be holding back from saying things that they or colleagues may find embarrassing, such as speaking up about a colleague who's behaving disrespectfully by interrupting or not listening to his peers. A management team can't improve its performance if managers are unwilling to raise issues that are affecting how they work together.

Take the lead by speaking up and expressing your views honestly and openly in your management meetings. (Turn to Chapter 5 for more information on speaking up.)

Expanding Your Sphere of Influence

Wouldn't your job be easier if you had total control over every aspect of your work! I doubt that you can achieve this desire but you can increase your influence with work colleagues who affect how well you're able to do your job. You may have to start with influencing how you think, however, before you're able to increase your influence over others.

Start to increase your influence by challenging your views about how much control you have over the people and other factors that affect your ability to do your job well: you probably have more influence than you think.

Identify the people with the biggest impact on your performance and invest time in working more closely with them to encourage and persuade them to do what you need them to do when you need it doing. (Chapter 4 provides guidance on increasing your sphere of influence.)

Chapter 14

Ten Tips for Engaging People

*L*eaders lead: followers choose to follow (or choose not to)! As a leader, you need to gain the commitment of your staff. This chapter contains tips on how to engage people so that they want to work with and for you, and do their jobs to the best of their ability.

Earning People's Respect

When some managers are promoted, power goes to their head: they seem to elevate themselves to a lofty position, look down on their work colleagues and tell them what to do. This behaviour tends to upset people who in turn lose respect for their manager.

 People choose to follow great leaders because they want to, not because they've been told to. You know that you're becoming a great leader when people enthusiastically do what you need them to do without you using your authority.

You can enthuse and encourage people so that they want to follow you in many different ways, and a good place to start is treating people with respect. (Chapter 1 contains more useful information on how to treat people correctly and so earn the right to lead them.)

Being Bolder

Setting relatively easy targets may give you confidence and comfort because you expect your team to achieve them, but you don't bring the best out of members of your team in this way. People apply their skills and talents more when they have to stretch themselves to achieve targets and need to get out of their comfort zone. (Turn to Chapter 2 for more on comfort zones.)

Be bold in setting and agreeing objectives and targets that stretch you and your team to make the greatest contribution you can to your organisation's success. (Chapter 4 contains lots more info in this area.)

Being bold can involve taking risks and you may, perhaps, feel uncomfortable because you're not certain of achieving demanding objectives and targets that you set yourself and your team. But playing safe means that you and your team are unlikely to perform to your full potential.

Making Things Meaningful

No doubt at times, as an employee or as a leader, you've questioned, at least in your own mind, the point or purpose of doing some tasks that you've been told to do. You know from experience that if you perceive certain work to be meaningless, you're unlikely to do it well: you may delay doing it because you have other priorities, rush through it just to get done, or simply not focus sufficiently and do a poor job. Similarly, you're unlikely fully to support a change introduced into your work area (such as a change in job roles and responsibilities, systems or procedures) when that change seems pointless.

You need to avoid your staff feeling this way. Hold conversations with work colleagues so they understand why you're asking them to do tasks or actively support a change that you intend to introduce. Better still, engage them in meaningful conversations so they can contribute their ideas and views, and question or even challenge your proposals in order to enhance your and their understanding of the issues and problems.

I propose that a better understanding of a problem is more likely to lead to a better decision being made and achieve a better outcome. (You can find much more on engaging people in meaningful conversations in Chapter 5.)

On certain occasions, such as when facing critical deadlines, you may be unable, or even not want, to involve everyone in a conversation about an issue: in such cases, you have to be decisive and instruct people to take action. But do explain your reasons for acting that way afterwards.

Striving to Gain Commitment

Employees have to comply by doing a good enough job to meet the requirements or expectations of their manager, and to avoid being disciplined. Of course most people do more than the minimum requirements, but everyone chooses whether to put in the extra effort to do outstanding work.

Ensure that all your team members choose to take ownership of their work and gain their commitment to do it to the best of their ability. Chapter 6 contains loads of great tips on being an engaging leader.

Always strive to gain the commitment of all your staff to do their work to the best of their ability, but ensure that at the very least people comply with your standards.

Getting the Most from Measurement

Many organisations invest a lot of time and effort in performance measurement/management and yet fail to achieve the best return on their investment in terms of improved performance. Reasons for not achieving the full benefits of performance measurement include the following:

- ✔ Appropriate measures haven't been identified.
- ✔ Appropriate key performance indicators (KPIs) aren't being used.
- ✔ KPIs are in conflict with each other.

Use performance measures such as KPIs effectively to ensure that they focus team members' attention on the right priorities and create an ethos of continuous improvement in your team. Chapters 4, 10 and 12 cover measuring performance, and Chapter 11 contains a section on continuous improvement.

Avoiding Being a Victim Of Change

You can't always choose the situations you find yourself in, but you can choose how you react to them. The rate of change seems to be increasing in all types of organisations due to the following:

- ✔ Advances in technology.
- ✔ Growth and globalisation of many businesses.
- ✔ Increasing competition.
- ✔ Greater customer expectations.

Such changes in your organisation can create considerable uncertainty for you and your staff.

Most of the change decisions that you're involved in or have to implement are probably made by more senior managers, and you may sometimes have to implement changes with which you disagree.

How you react in these situations is critical because your reaction has a significant impact on the people who report to you.

Avoid being a 'victim of change' and thinking that you can't do anything about these changes: you do at least choose how you communicate and introduce changes to your staff. Maintain a positive influence on how change is introduced into your workplace and look for ways in which you can increase your sphere of influence. (Flip to Chapter 4 for guidance on how to be an agent of change and increase your sphere of influence.)

Celebrating People's Contributions

Quite naturally, leaders focus on the future especially during times of rapid change. Leaders have to be forward-thinking to set the direction of their company or team, and gain the commitment of everyone to go in the chosen direction. However, by focusing on the future, leaders can sometimes forget to acknowledge important aspects of the past.

One issue that many leaders overlook is the contribution that people have made to getting the organisation or team to where it is now. Employees who think that they've made an important contribution to past success can feel demoralised when their past contribution is overlooked, perhaps because the precious work was for another leader.

Celebrate the contribution that people have made and are making to the success of your team and/or organisation. (Chapters 9 and 10 contain much more on leading change.)

Striking While the Iron's Hot

Some managers have good intentions to raise a team member's under-performance or unacceptable behaviour, but somehow never get round to it. Reasons for procrastinating can include the following:

- ✔ The manager is unsure how to raise the topic.
- ✔ The manager isn't assertive enough.
- ✔ The manager thinks that other priorities are more pressing.

In my experience, managerial inactivity tends to contribute to the person's behaviour or performance deteriorating further. Chapter 8 covers promoting and reinforcing your standards and working with colleagues to improve their behaviour and performance.

Act promptly – 'while the iron's hot' – when raising any instances of people not behaving or performing to your standards in order to reinforce the standards you expect.

Making a Good Team Great

I've witnessed many teams that believe they're performing pretty well and think that they're already a good team. The truth is that most teams I encounter are doing a reasonable job, but my concern is that teams that believe they're good also think that they've no need to improve. These teams tend to stop the journey towards being a great team before even starting out.

Constructively question and challenge your team, and any team you belong to for that matter, about how good it really is. Ask team members to clarify the benchmark or criteria they're using to assess how good the team is and how well it performs. (Chapter 11 describes the characteristics of great teams, and how to conduct team assessments.)

Creating Time for Coaching

Organisations are increasingly recognising that coaching is a very effective way of developing the knowledge, skills, attitude and performance of employees. Many companies are employing external coaches to work with their senior leaders to enable them to enhance their leadership ability and performance, and to become competent in coaching the people who work for them.

Invest time in developing your coaching skills, and then make time to coach each person who reports directly to you so they can enhance their skills and improve their performance. Coaching your direct reports benefits you as well as them because you can delegate some of your work and responsibilities, and free up more time to focus on other priorities.

Don't limit yourself to coaching only those people reporting directly to you: make time to informally coach your peers and even your boss! You need to be tactful as well as use current relevant evidence of unacceptable behaviour or performance when coaching people who don't report to you if you expect them to improve their performance. Chapter 8 contains useful information on making coaching part of your everyday leadership practice.

Index

FOR DUMMIES®

Making Everything Easier!™

UK editions

BUSINESS

978-0-470-74490-1

978-0-470-74381-2

978-0-470-71025-8

REFERENCE

978-0-470-68637-9

978-0-470-97450-6

978-0-470-74535-9

HOBBIES

978-0-470-69960-7

978-0-470-68641-6

978-0-470-68178-7

Anger Management
For Dummies
978-0-470-68216-6

Asperger's Syndrome
For Dummies
978-0-470-66087-4

Boosting Self-Esteem
For Dummies
978-0-470-74193-1

British Sign Language
For Dummies
978-0-470-69477-0

Cricket For Dummies
978-0-470-03454-5

Diabetes For Dummies,
3rd Edition
978-0-470-97711-8

Emotional Healing
For Dummies
978-0-470-74764-3

English Grammar
For Dummies
978-0-470-05752-0

Flirting For Dummies
978-0-470-74259-4

Football For Dummies
978-0-470-68837-3

Healthy Mind & Body All-in-One
For Dummies
978-0-470-74830-5

IBS For Dummies
978-0-470-51737-6

Improving Your Relationship
For Dummies
978-0-470-68472-6

Nutrition For Dummies,
2nd Edition
978-0-470-97276-2

FOR DUMMIES®

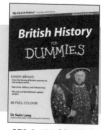

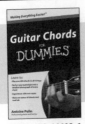

FOR DUMMIES®

Helping you expand your horizons and achieve your potential

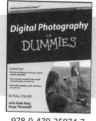
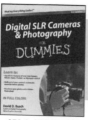